ESSENTIAL OILS FOR DOGS

A Practical Guide to Healing Your Dog Faster, Cheaper and Safer with the Power of Essential Oils

By Mary Jones

Copyright© 2016 by Mary Jones - All rights reserved.

Copyright: No part of this publication may be reproduced without written permission from the author, except by a reviewer who may quote brief passages or reproduce illustrations in a review with appropriate credits; nor may any part of this book be reproduced, stored in a retrieval system, or transmitted in any form or by any means – electronic, mechanical, photocopying, recording, or other - without prior written permission of the copyright holder.

The trademarks are used without any consent, and the publication of the trademark is without permission or backing by the trademark owner. All trademarks and brands within this book are for clarifying purposes only and are owned by the owners themselves.

Disclaimer: The information in this book is not to be used as Veterinary medical advice and is not meant to treat or diagnose animal medical problems. The information presented should be used in combination with guidance from your Veterinarian.

The information in this book is true and complete to the best of our knowledge. All recommendations are made without guarantee on the part of the author. It is the sole responsibility of the reader to educate and train in the use of all or any specialized equipment that may be used or referenced in this book that could cause harm or injury to the user or applicant. The author disclaims any liability in connection with the use of this information. References are provided for informational purposes only and do not constitute endorsement of any websites or other sources. Readers should be aware that the websites listed in this book may change.

First Printing, 2016 - Printed in the United States of America

*"The therapeutic benefits of essential oils
are meant for **every** member of the family, including DOGS…"*

- Cesar Millan (Dog Trainer)

TABLE OF CONTENTS

Introduction	1
A Quick Guide to Essential Oils	3
Brief History	5
The Ways Essential Oils Work	7
Top 5 Reasons to Use Essential Oils	9
3 Proven Steps for Buying Essential Oils	11
A Quick Reference Guide to Botanical Names	15
Advanced Ways to Dilute Essential Oils	23
9 Little Secrets for Storing Essential Oils	29
Safety Precautions That You Should Know	31
Best Application Techniques	39
5 Ultimate Steps for Blending Essential Oils	43
8 Tested Blending Tips	49
Top 4 Insider Tips for Using Essential Oils with Dogs	51
Essential Oils to Consider	55
Top 30 Essential Oils for the Betterment of Your Dog	56
27 Risky Essential Oils to Avoid for Your Dog	115
Steps to Take if You Suspect Poisoning	117

40 Little Known Essential Oil Recipes	119
Essential Oils for Common Dog Ailments	163
Recap - Top 20 Tips for Essential Oils Use with Dogs	167
FAQ	171
Resources	177
Conclusion	183
About the Author	185

INTRODUCTION

Are you concerned about your dog's health?

Our pets very quickly become our best friend and a member of the family, and for that reason we *only* want to treat them with the best! Studies have shown that **one of the most common worries for dog owners** is being able to provide the best healing and disease prevention and that is just one of the many reasons why more and more **people are turning to alternative therapies – such as essential oils** – to achieve this.

There are a great number of **benefits to using these essential oils** in the everyday healthcare of your pet that you just cannot get with traditional medicine. A few of which are listed below:

- **Non toxic** – these oils are all natural, there is nothing toxic that can harm your dog (only if used correctly)
- **Easy to use** – they can be inhaled or placed on your dog's body, at home or wherever you are.
- **Easy to make** – you can blend your own, so you know *exactly* what is going into them.
- **Helpful with training** – great for the emotional side of training also.

As stated by Dog Fun Times Guide (dogs.thefuntimesguide.com), *"Truth be told, you can't hurt anything by trying!"*

But the problem is **a lot of people just do not know where to start!**

That's where this guide comes in. Not only will it give you comprehensive information to buying the right oils, it will also give you details on how to use them, where to apply them and what oils to avoid among many other useful facts. You won't be able to find another book on the market that gives you as much information as this one does. Not only will it answer *all* of your questions, it will direct you to some brilliant resources to get even more information once you have finished reading.

Once you get to the end of this book, you'll know all that you need to, to start using these oils with your own pets. You'll have extensive knowledge on what to buy and also how to create your own oils in your kitchen. **Your dog will never have to suffer a common ailment without treatment again!**

A QUICK GUIDE TO ESSENTIAL OILS

Essential oils are described as follows:

"The volatile liquids that are distilled from plants including their respective parts such as seeds, bark, leaves, stems, roots, flowers, fruit, etc. An essential oil contains the true essence of the plant it was derived from and is highly concentrated. Essential oils, contrary to the use of the word "oil" are not really oily-feeling at all. Most essential oils are clear although some oils are amber or yellow in color."

A single essential oil is processed from one plant species. It contains only the constituents of that particular plant and is very direct in its effectiveness regarding healing. **A blended essential oil** contains a variety of single essential oils that are placed together to formulate a unique blend.

What you might not know about essential oils is *they aren't actually oils*! They don't contain any of the fatty acids that constitute what we would consider an oil.

Brief History

From all the records available, it seems that the Egyptians were the first people to use aromatic herbs and essential oils for religious as well as medicinal purposes. They are thought to have developed the distillation method which is still used to extract essential oils today. This system was passed down until it reached the Peruvian physician named *Avicenna* who is credited for perfecting it in approximately 1,000AD.

During this time, animals have used these oils as much as humans. As stated by Jean Pierre Hourdebaigt (jeanpierrehourdebaigt.com/essential-oils-for-animals), who has written extensively on the subject, *"Due to the physiological similarities animals react in similar ways to essential oils."* This suggests that the makeup of humans and animals means that we can all benefit from this form of medication. The website goes on further to suggest that humans have a *"preconceived idea about the oils"*, which can affect their effectiveness, that animals do not.

THE WAYS ESSENTIAL OILS WORK

The way these oils work on animals is very similar to humans. Essential oils work through body chemistry and the nervous system.

1. Body Chemistry

When essential oils are absorbed through the skin, they are working directly through our body chemistry affecting systems of the body. Each plant extract has chemical properties that are distinctive such as anti-inflammatory or cell rejuvenation. Tiny molecules of essential oils are easily absorbed by the membranes of the lungs and through skin pores and hair follicles. The chemical constituents/properties of the oils are carried in the bloodstream to all areas of the body. Essential oils bring on gentle physiological change.

2. Nervous System

Essential oils can have a healing effect both mentally and emotionally. The psychological benefits are usually obtained when essential oils are inhaled. Our sense of smell is governed by the olfactory organ at the top of our nose. Tiny cilia and receptor cells have direct access to the brain. The aroma sends an immediate signal to the limbic system of the brain. The limbic system is the center of memory and emotion. The oils can exert a powerful effect on mind, mood, and emotions.

A study conducted by Wells in 2006 (thebark.com/content/essential-oils-and-dogs) demonstrates **how these essential oils work on dogs**: Essential oils are aromatic, naturally occurring chemical components of plants that are usually extracted by distillation. Thorough lab testing of these chemical constituents has led to an understanding of their benefits, and in recent years, interest in therapeutically blended essential oils for canines has increased.

TOP 5 REASONS TO USE ESSENTIAL OILS

Essential oils can enter the body in one of three ways:

- Applied to the skin
- Inhaled
- Ingested

The oil is then absorbed and gets to work. This isn't much different for animals – and in particular, dogs, although the topical method is the most common used. They also work on a lot of the same ailments; for example anxiety, stomach upset and headaches. This book is going to go into much more detail about which oils are best for which ailment, and how to administer them with dogs.

Some studies conducted have found that dogs respond really well to home remedies, in particular the ones that use essential oils. The **list of benefits** it gives are:

1. They aren't toxic, so are safe to use (only if used correctly).
2. They are much easier to use with your pet than traditional medicine.
3. You can administer them at home.
4. They can travel with you everywhere you go.
5. They can be used to cure or prevent a lot of diseases!

Of course, there are also **some negative points when it comes to essential oils**, and these must be considered too when taking the choice to use them. The most prominent are:

- There isn't the same *regulation* as traditional medicine.

- *Limited research* – although there is more being conducted all the time.
- As with all medication, the *side effects* can vary so it's best to be aware of this.

When it comes to using essential oils with animals, most of the negative effects come from human error, so it's best to ensure that you have all the information on hand before starting to use them. There are many useful online resources when it comes to safety – so there is no reason not to be suitably informed.

3 PROVEN STEPS FOR BUYING ESSENTIAL OILS

When buying essential oils, there are a few things you will want to consider. The most important being:

1. *What am I using the oil for?*
2. *What is the grade of oil needed?*
3. *What is the grade of oil wanted?*

It is difficult to make a decision on this, without **understanding the oil 'grades'** and what they mean. As there is no one regulating body for these oils, this grade chart has been created to help buyers know exactly what it is they're getting. Note, that no government agency or generally accepted organization "grades" or "certifies" essential oils as "therapeutic grade", "medicinal grade", or "aromatherapy grade" in the US. There is no formally approved grading standard used consistently throughout the essential oil industry so the chart below is only provided for informational purposes.

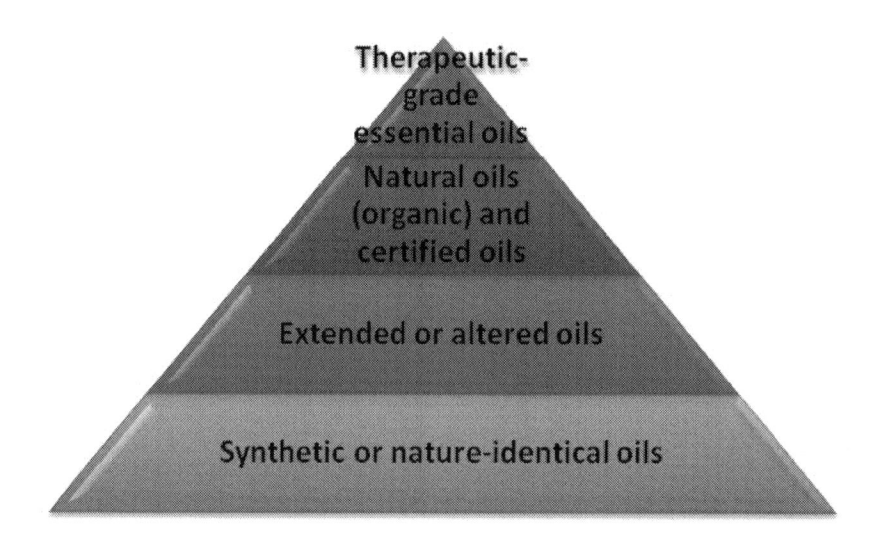

```
                    Therapeutic-
                       grade
                   essential oils
                    Natural oils
                   (organic) and
                    certified oils

               Extended or altered oils

           Synthetic or nature-identical oils
```

Therapeutic-grade essential oils	Pure, medicinal, steam-distilled essential oils containing all desired therapeutic compounds
Natural oils (organic) and certified oils	Pass oil-standard tests but may not contain any or just a few therapeutic compounds
Extended or altered oils	Fragrance grade
Synthetic or nature-identical oils	Created in a laboratory

It is important to remember the **difference between 'pure' and 'quality'** essential oils when buying. Pure means undiluted, whereas quality refers to how well the product is made. There can be a bad quality oil, that's pure. For more information about pure and quality oils, check out the NAHA website at www.naha.org.

Obviously, in the case of this guide, you will be using the oils for your dog. When it comes to animals, the **recommendation is to go with 100% therapeutic grade**. Though these terms can be misleading, not all companies use these terms with intentional deception in mind.

There are many factors that make therapeutic grade essential oil, but all of them really fit into two main categories.

- *Environmental Factors*– Where the plant is grown; the soil type; fertilizer (organic vs. chemical); altitude, etc.
- *Physical Factors*– How and when the plant is harvested, how it is distilled and even how it is bottled.

These therapeutic grade oils meet stringent distillation and testing procedures and are produced with no solvents. They are costly to produce which means there aren't many high quality producers, but a little research will lead you to a reputable company. If you come across the company that uses the term *aromatherapy grade* or *therapeutic grade*, look for other key indicators of the essential oil quality and attempt to asses their particular intent in behind their use of the term. Some companies provide details on their site that define their particular use of the term. Whilst some companies do use these terms in a manner that is intentionally misleading consumers.

It may surprise you to learn exactly **how many plants are needed to produce essential oil**. In fact, on the extreme end, it takes 4000 pounds of Bulgarian roses to produce 1 pound of essential oil. Or a drop of peppermint essential oil is equal t 26 cups of peppermint tea. This just shows how much work and material is needed to make this, which is why a number of people believe that the higher the price of the product, the better the quality will be. (Quality is not to be confused with 'pure' which means nothing has been added to the project).

You can always judge the quality for yourself by researching company's standards. The choice is yours but it's always recommended to discuss anything you use with a professional.

So now that you know the grade you need, we need to focus on the product required. Of course, that entirely depends on the ailment your dog is suffering from, so we will go into much more detail about this throughout the rest of this book, but below is a short guide from Young Living (www.youngliving.com) to get you started.

Everyday Oils for Pets

www.thegoodoil.webs.com

FRANKINCENSE: Safer, gentle oil that is a favorite for smaller pets and birds. Used in every aspect of pet care: wounds, tumors, behavior, infections, bacterial and fungal control. Dilution recommended with lavender.

LEMON: Used to increase awareness in training or cognitive issues. It is an anti-parasitic and can be combined with others safely, excellent for skin conditions. Use topically, diffused or ingested.

LAVENDER: Use for injuries while hiking or riding. Gentle but anti-infectious. When combined with peppermint, healing is increased and infection and pain is decreased. Repels parasites and calms nervous system. May be helpful for masses and tumors.

PEPPERMINT: Use with PanAway for any injury. Most used oil for overheated horses and dogs, provides cooling quickly. Used on long hikes, place a drop in water for internal cooling. Peppermint must be diluted for cats, 1 part oil to 4 parts vegetable oil.

PANAWAY: Best oil blend for injury. Can be used with cats if diluted. Used for urinary issues, osteo-arthritis pain, dental extraction or post-surgery. Use topically in warm compress, in raindrop technique or vita-flex points on feet.

PEACE & CALMING: Main calming blend of this collection. Use for fear, anxiety, behavior problems, car rides, excitement. Builds confidence.

PURIFICATION: Use for parasites such as fleas, ticks and mosquitos for dog and horse. Dilute 75% for cats. For birds, mist the cage with oil instead of applying directly to the bird.

THIEVES: Strongest anti-infectious blend in this collection. Can be used on all pets if diluted properly. Provides significant pain relief, particularly for dental problems. Has anti-parasitic properties, especially for ticks. Can be used topically to location of injury, vita-flex, raindrop, or internally. Diffuse

VALOR: Useful for all pets for fear, behavior and training. Especially useful for pet rescue. Use for skin masses, itching, allergies and infections. Diffuse or apply topically. Place around collar or leash.

A QUICK REFERENCE GUIDE TO BOTANICAL NAMES

Many experts in the use of essential oils suggest that you have a much better chance of buying the best quality, if you have a good knowledge of the botanical names associated with ingredients. You can keep the chart below as a reference guide to ensure you're constantly in the know.

Oil	Botanical Name
Ambrette Seed	Hibiscus abelmoschus
Angelica	Angelica archangelica
Anise	Pimpinella anisum
Atlas Cedar	Cedrus atlantica
Balsam Copaiba	Copaifera officinalis
Balsam Peru	Myroxylon pereirae
Balsam Tolu	Myroxylon balsamum
Bay Laurel	Laurus nobilis
Basil	Ocimum basilicum var.Linalool
Benzoin	Styrax benzoin
Bergamot	Citrus bergamia
Bergamot Mint	Mentha citrate
Black Pepper	Piper nigrum
Blue Tansy	Tanacetum annuum
Camphor White	Cinnamomum camphora (Bark)
Cardamom	Elettaria cardamomum
Carrot	Daucua carota
Cassia	Cinnamomum cassia
Cedar Red	Thuja plicata
Cedar Leaf (Thuja)	Thuja occidentalis

ESSENTIAL OILS FOR DOGS

Cedarwood (Atlas Cedar)	Cedrus atlantica
Chamomile Cape	Eriocephalus punctulatus
Chamomile German (Blue)	Matricaria recutita or Chamaemelum matricaria
Chamomile Morrocan (Blue Tansy)	Tanacetum annuum
Chamomile Roman	Anthemis nobilis or Chamaemelum nobile
Cinnamon Bark	Cinnamomum verum
Cinnamon Leaf	Cinnamomum zeylanicum
Cistus (Labdanum) (Rock Rose)	Cistus ladaniferus
Citronella	Cymbopogon nardus
Clary Sage	Salvia sclarea
Clove	Syzygium aromaticum
Cocoa	Theobroma cacao
Coriander	Coriandrum savitum
Cumin	Cuminum cyminum
Cypress	Cupressus sempervirens
Cypress Blue	Callitris intratropica
Davana	Artemisia pallens
Elemi	Canarium luzonicum
Eucalyptus	Eucalyptus globules
Eucalyptus Lemon	Eucalyptus citriodora
Eucalyptus Radiata	Eucalyptus radiate

Eucalyptus Staigeriana or Balm	Eucalyptus Staigeriana
Fennel	Foeniculum vulgare
Fir Balsam	Abies balsamea
Fir Silver	Abies alba
Fir Douglas	Pseudotsuga menziesii
Fir Grand	Abies grandis
Frankincense (Olibanum)	Boswellia carterii or serrata or frareana
Galbanum	Ferula gummosa
Geranium	Pelargonium graveolens
Ginger	Zingiber officinale
Grapefruit	Citrus paradisii
Helichrysum (Everlasting or Immortelle)	Helichrysum italicum
Hyssop	Hyssopus officinalis
Inula	Inula graveolens
Jasmine	Jasminum officinale
Juniper Berry	Juniperus communis
Khella	Amni visnaga
Kunzea	Kunzea ambigua
Lavender	Lavandula angustifolia or officinale
Lavendin	Lavandula x hybrid
Lemon	Citrus limonum
Lemon Myrtle	Backhousia citriodora

ESSENTIAL OILS FOR DOGS

Lemon Tea Tree	Leptospermum petersonii
Lemon Verbena (Vervaine)	Aloysia citriodora
Lemongrass	Cymbopogon flexuosus
Lime	Citrus aurantifolia
Linden Blossom	Tilia cordata
Litsea (May Chang)	Litsea cubeba
Lotus White	Nymphaea lotus
Mandarin	Citrus reticulata or deliciosa
Manuka (New Zealand Tea Tree)	Leptospermum scoparium
Mastick	Lentiscus pistachius
May Chang	Litsea cubeba
Melissa (Lemon Balm)	Melissa officinalis
Marjoram	Origanum majorana
Mimosa	Acacia dealbata
Monarda (Bee Balm)	Monarda fistulosa
MQV (niaouli nerol type AKA Nerolina)	Melaleuca quinquenervia veridiflora
Myrrh	Commiphora myrrha
Myrtle	Myrtus communis
Myrtle Lemon	Backhousia citriodora
Neroli (Orange Blossom)	Citrus aurantium var. Amara

Nerolina	Melaleuca quinquenervia veridiflora
Niaouli	Melaleuca quinquenervia
Nutmeg	Myristica fragrans
Orange	Citrus sinensis
Oregano	Origanum vulgare var.Carvacrol
Owyhee	Artemesia ludoviciana
Palmarosa	Cymbopogon martini
Patchouli	Pogostemon cablin
Pepper Black	Piper nigrum
Peppermint	Mentha piperita
Petitgrain Bigarade	Citrus aurantium var.Amara
Pine Sylvester (Scotch Pine)	Pinus sylvestris
Ravensara	Ravensara aromatic
Ravintsara	Cinnamomum camphora (Leaf)
Rock Rose (Cistus) (Labdanum)	Cistus ladaniferus
Rosalina (Lavender Tea Tree)	Melaleuca ericifolia
Rose Damask (Otto)	Rosa damascene
Rose Moroc	Rosa centifolia
Rosemary	Rosmarinus officinalis
Rosemary Verbenone	Rosmarinus officinalis var.Verbenon
Rosewood	Aniba rosaeodora

ESSENTIAL OILS FOR DOGS

Sage	Salvia officinalis
Sandalwood Australian	Santalum spicatum
Sandalwood Indian	Santalum album
Spearmint	Mentha spicata
Spikenard	Nardostachys jatamansi
Spruce Black	Picea mariana
St Johnswort	Hypericum perforatum
Tamanu (Foraha)	Calophyllum inophyllum
Tangerine	Citrus reticulata or nobilis
Tansy Blue	Tanacetum annuum
Tarragon	Artemisia dracunculus
Tea Tree	Melaleuca alternifolia
Tea Tree Lavender (Rosalina)	Melaleuca ericifolia
Tea Tree Lemon	Leptospermum petersonii
Tea Tree New Zealand (Manuka)	Leptospermum scoparium
Thyme Linalool	Thymus vulgaris var.Linalool
Valerian	Valeriana officinalis
Vanilla	Vanilla planifolia
Vervaine (Lemon Verbena)	Aloysia citriodora
Vetiver	Vetiveria zizanoides
Violet Leaf	Viola odorata

Vitex	Vitex agnus castus
White Lotus	Nymphaea lotus
Wintergreen	Gaultheria procumbens
Yarrow	Achillea millefolium
Ylang Ylang	Cananga odorata var. Genuana
Vanilla	Vanilla planifolia
Vervaine (Lemon Verbena)	Aloysia citriodora
Vetiver	Vetiveria zizanoides
Violet Leaf	Viola odorata
Vitex	Vitex agnus castus
White Lotus	Nymphaea lotus
Wintergreen	Gaultheria procumbens
Yarrow	Achillea millefolium
Ylang Ylang	Cananga odorata var. Genuana

So now that you have a little idea about buying essential oils – something that you'll become much more familiar with through the rest of the book – it's time to hit you with another little known fact. According to some sources, **essential oils should last for at least 5 years** (if not 10), so one bottle could literally last you a decade. Hopefully that thought will help mitigate the cost involved in purchasing some essential oils. Because they are *so* concentrated and only a tiny amount is needed in anything you do, they'll last you a very, very long time. The only exception to this rule is citrus oils, which will see a reduction in potency after a year or two. Please note however once mixed with carrier oil, the blend is only valid while the carrier oil is good.

ADVANCED WAYS TO DILUTE ESSENTIAL OILS

Another thing you need to be aware of is dilution. Because essential oils are so concentrated, they need to be diluted so that they're safe to apply. The best way to achieve this is via **carrier oil**. As your carrier oil, select a high quality vegetable oil, preferably one that has been cold pressed. Example carrier oils include coconut, almond, apricot, olive, macadamia or sesame. Carrier oils should be stored away from heat and light to ensure their freshness.

Usually there are following main *distillation methods*:

Water Distillation – This method is where the plant material is placed in boiling water. The steam and oils are captured and then separated out to produce the essential oil.

Water/Steam Distillation – This method is where steam and water are pushed around and though the plant material. And then the steam and oils are captured and then separated out to produce the essential oil.

Straight Steam Distillation – Distilling essential oils using the straight steam method involves pushing steam through the plant material and then picking up the essential oil.

Cold Pressed – This is considered by WH Foods (www.whfoods.com) to be the healthiest way to distil oil: The oil is obtained through pressing and grinding fruit or seeds with the use of heavy granite millstones or modern stainless steel presses, which are found in large commercial operations. Although pressing and grinding produces heat through friction, the temperature must not rise above 120°F (49°C) for any oil to be considered cold pressed. Cold pressed oils are produced at even lower temperatures. Cold pressed oils retain all of their flavor, aroma, and nutritional value. Olive, peanut and sunflower are among the oils that are obtained through cold pressing.

In all of the methods, steam is used to rupture the oil membranes in the plant and release the essential oil. The steam carries the essential oil to a condenser and then as it re-liquefies the lighter essential oil floats on top. The water and oil are then separated out, and the water is referred to as the *hydrosol* or *hydrolat*, or flower or *floral water*. And the oil of course is the essential oil.

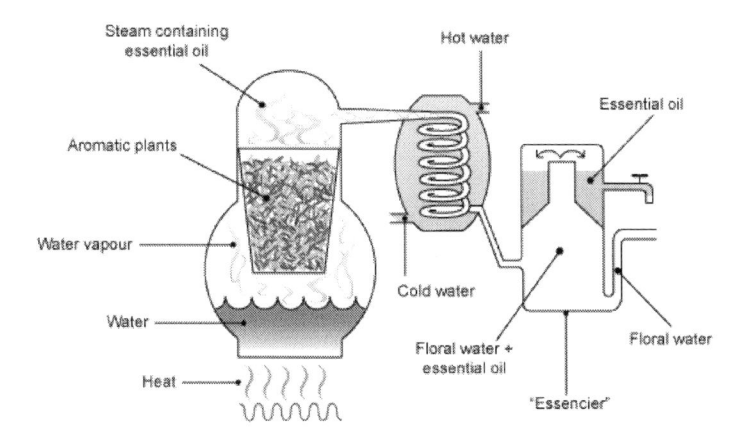

The chart below indicates the **most effective ratios to use to dilute essential oils**:

Essential Oil Dilution Chart

nourishingtreasures.com/EOdilutions

Dilution	1%	2%	3%	5%	10%	25%
drops of EO for **1 tsp** (5ml; 1/6 oz.) carrier oil	1	2	3	5	10	25
drops of EO for **2 tsp** (10ml; 1/3 oz.) carrier oil	2	4	6	10	20	50
drops of EO for **3 tsp** (15ml; 1/2 oz.) carrier oil	3	6	9	15	30	75
drops of EO for **4 tsp** (20ml; 2/3 oz.) carrier oil	4	8	12	20	40	100
drops of EO for **5 tsp** (25ml; 5/6 oz.) carrier oil	5	10	15	25	50	125
drops of EO for **6 tsp** (30ml; 1 oz.) carrier oil	6	12	18	30	60	150

Another way to look at this is the *Essential Oils Measurement Equivalents chart*:

- 100 drops = 1 tsp = 5ml = 1/6 ounce
- 200 drops = 2 tsp = 10ml = 1/3 ounce
- 300 drops = 3 tsp = 15ml = 1/2 ounce
- 400 drops = 4 tsp = 20ml = 2/3 ounce
- 500 drops = 5 tsp = 25ml = 5/6 ounce
- 600 drops = 6 tsp = 30ml = 1 ounce

It's important to bear in mind that there *are* a few essential oils that are generally recognized as safe to use undiluted. Of course, there has to be a few exceptions to the rule. According to Crunchy Betty (www.crunchybetty.com), the only **essential oils that are widely acknowledged as safe to use undiluted** (sparingly) are: *Lavender, German chamomile, Sandalwood,* and *Rose geranium.*

When it comes to dogs, the **dilution ratio is based mostly on the size of the dog**, as shown below:

Small dogs, 5-15 lb, would have a 90% dilution with essential oil application (i.e. 1 drop of essential oil diluted with 10 drops of carrier oil)

Small-Medium dogs, 16-40 lb, would have a 75% dilution used (1 drop of essential oil to 4 drops of carrier oil)

Medium dogs, 41-75 lb, would have a 50% dilution of the essential oil

Medium-Large dogs, 76-90 lb, would have a 25-50% dilution of the essential oil.

Large dogs, 91-150 lb, would have a 25% dilution.

Extra large dogs, 150 lb and up, would have a 0-25% dilution.

You also need to **take the dog's age into considerations**. Below are recommendations:

1% dilution is recommended for *very young* and *very old dogs*.

3% – 10% dilution is best *for short-term use*, for a temporary health issue.

25% dilution is occasionally warranted *for severe issues*.

Always discuss this information with a health professional.

You should use with caution or heavily dilute for pregnant dogs, old, sick; dogs prone to seizures!

> # Dilute, Dilute, Dilute!
> LearningAboutEOs.com/dilute
>
> Concentrated substances are rarely intended for use "as is" - and essential oils are no different. There is almost never a time when you would not want to dilute the potency of an essential oil.
>
> Diluting essential oils is done by adding a drop (or more) of the essential oil into a carrier oil. This not only provides a good medium for the oil to absorb into the skin, but spreads the oil over a larger surface of your skin for more effect.

This demonstrates the general rule used. It is recommended to **start with a higher dilution** than less, because dogs can't talk and *tell* you how they're reacting to their oils so you will have to keep an eye on them and judge for yourself. You can increase the dilution rate if you see your pet taking to the essential oils in a positive way.

9 LITTLE SECRETS FOR STORING ESSENTIAL OILS

The final thing we need to look at in this chapter of the book is storage. The way you look after your essential oils *will* affect their shelf life, so it's important to follow the correct procedure to save yourself time, money and effort. Below is a great 'do's and don'ts' guide:

1. *Don't* expose your essential oils to extreme or rapid changes in temperature.
2. *Do* keep your essential oils packaged in dark, colored glass because this filters out the suns UV rays.
3. *Do* keep your essential oils stored in a cool, dark place.
4. *Do* use the refrigerator to store your essential oils if you have the space.
5. *Don't* let your carrier oils get too warm as this will compromise the quality of the essential oils.
6. *Do* consider using an aromatherapy box if you don't have the room in your refrigerator. These are specifically designed to keep your essential oils at the desired temperature.
7. *Do* replace the cap of your essential oil bottles immediately after you have finished using them. They are prone to evaporating and you don't want to risk losing them in this way.
8. *Don't* ever leave your essential oils near naked flame as they are highly flammable materials.
9. *Don't* ever decant your essential oils into plastic bottles as they will likely melt through it.

You may know that most essential oils are high in antibacterial, antifungal, and antiviral properties, but did you also know that **essential oils are wholly natural and cannot be patented**; which means that you'll never see an essential oil in a pharmaceutical drug.

This may also go some way to explain why a lot of health professionals don't automatically recommend them as a solution, and also why companies don't want to spend money into researching the benefits – when they can't directly reap the benefits of their studies.

SAFETY PRECAUTIONS THAT YOU SHOULD KNOW

One of the most important things to think about when coming to essential oil use is safety. Safety involves a state of being free from risk or occurrence of injury, harm, or danger. *The National Association for Holistic Aromatherapy* (www.naha.org) has an extensive guide on this topic. Now, not all of this will apply to animals, but it's best to be aware of *all* the guidelines in place so you can protect yourself too – as you will be the one administering the essential oils.

Factors that influence the safety of essential oils include:

1. *Quality of essential oil being utilized* – Adulterated essential oils increase the likelihood of an adverse response and hence the need for pure, authentic, and genuine essential oils is of the utmost importance.
2. *Chemical composition of the oil* – Essential oils rich in aldehydes (e.g., citronellal, citral) and phenols (e.g., cinnamic aldehyde, eugenol) may cause reactions. Essential oils rich in these constituents should always be diluted prior to application.
3. *Method of application* – Essential oils may be applied topically, inhaled, diffused or taken internally. Each of these methods have safety issues which need to be considered.
4. *Dosage/dilution to be applied* – Most aromatherapy oil based blends will be between 1 and 5 percent dilutions, which typically does not represent a safety concern. As one increases dilution, potential reactions may take place depending on the individual essential oil, the area in which the oil is applied, and other factors related to the users own sensitivity levels.
5. *Integrity of area the oil is to be applied* – Damaged, diseased, or inflamed

skin is often more permeable to essential oils and may be more sensitive to dermal reactions. It is potentially dangerous to put undiluted essential oils on to damaged, diseased or inflamed skin. Under these circumstances the skin condition may be worsened, and larger amounts of oil than normal will be absorbed. Sensitization reactions are also more likely to occur.
6. *Age of client* – Very young and very old are more sensitive to the potency of essential oils.

You need to **be particularly careful when it comes to skin and eyes.** If any area becomes irritated, blotchy, red, suffers a burning sensation or displays *any* unusual symptoms due to the essential oils, it is recommended that you seek medical assistance. The same goes for *any* reaction if the oils come into contact with your pet's eyes; wash it out as much as possible, then speak to a veterinarian.

A study conducted by *Tiny Burnfield* in 2004 (*shown at the NAHA website at www.naha.org*) suggests that care needs to be taken with **essential oil use when pregnant** because of the oil constitutes crossing over into the placenta *"to my thinking the responsible attitude is to discourage the use of essential oils completely during the first few months of pregnancy"*. This *may* not cause you any issues, but it is best to check with your doctor before handling the oils and using them with your pet.

General Safety Precautions:

1. Keep all essential oils stored out of reach of children and pets.
2. Do not use or recommend the use of photosensitizing essential oils prior to going into the sun. Keep your dog out of the sun for at least twenty-four hours after treatment if photosensitizing essential oils were applied.
3. Avoid prolonged use of the same essential oils.
4. Avoid the use of essential oils you know nothing about on your pets. Research and get to know the oil prior to using it.
5. Avoid the use of undiluted essential oils, unless otherwise indicated.
6. If you suspect your dog may be sensitive to specific essential oils or if your pet has known allergies or sensitivities, it may be wise to perform a patch test.
7. Know the safety data on each essential oil and place into context of use and knowledge.
8. Keep essential oils away from the eyes.
9. Essential oils are highly flammable substances and should be kept away from direct contact with flames, such as candles, fire, matches, cigarettes, and gas cookers.
10. Make sure your treatment room has good ventilation.
11. Do not use essential oils internally unless properly trained in the safety issues of doing so.

Safety Measures:

1. If essential oil droplets accidentally get into the eye a cotton cloth or similar should be imbued with a fatty oil, such as olive or sesame, and carefully swiped over the closed lid and / or, immediately flush the eyes with cool water.
2. If an essential oil causes irritation, apply a small amount of vegetable oil or cream to the area affected and discontinue use of essential oil or product that has caused dermal irritation.
3. If your pet appears to have drunk several spoonfuls of essential oil, contact the nearest poison control unit e.g. Pet Poison Helpline (www.petpoisonhelpline.com, 800-213-6680). Keep the bottle for identification.

NAHA Animal Safety Precautions:

- Do not use essential oils with the following:
- Cats/Felines due to their highly sensitive metabolic systems, cats and essential oils do not mix.
- Fish and reptiles due to their pH levels and aquatic environments.
- Birds due to their respiratory and metabolic systems.
- Pet rodents and small mammals (gerbils, hamsters, rabbits, rats etc.) There is not enough research on this topic, other than actual animal-testing and research results gained for knowledge use with humans.

Essential oils for use with animals may include the following *safe methods of application*:

- Inhalation.
- Diffusion (avoid use near fish tanks or any bird's cage/area).
- Topical (spot application, massage therapy, bathing).

Safety Precautions and Contraindications for Animals:

- Animals will often lick the area where essential oil blends/botanicals have been applied. This normally does not cause a problem – but watch to make sure that the animal does not have an allergic reaction, or negative response. If they do, wipe the area with a cool wet cloth and diluted mild soap, rinse and repeat. If necessary seek immediate veterinarian assistance.
- Other and more serious clinical signs to watch for with your pet that can result from ingestion of essential oils are: vomiting, diarrhea, depression, lethargy, weakness, excessive drooling/salivation, mouth sores, seizures, tremors, increase in liver enzymes and temporary paralysis.
- Never apply essential oils directly to an animal's muzzle area, inside nostrils, ears or mouth, and genital areas.
- Do not force essential oils onto animals by way of a head or muzzle mask breather-type device/gear.
- If irritation occurs (this can happen via topical, diffusion and inhalation) discontinue use of essential oils and re-evaluate. If animal has a coughing or breathing issue due to the aromas, remove the animal from the area and, if symptoms persist or get worse, contact your veterinarian.
- Do not apply essential oils neat (undiluted) to animals. Essential oils should always be diluted when applied topically to animals. Over-use of essential oils and neat applications can cause sensitization issues.
- There are certain essential oils that should not be used with animals: one in particular is **Tea tree** (*Melaleuca alternifolia*), which for some pets can cause poisoning and other serious health concerns.
- Remember: **Less is best** with essential oil use, do not be tempted to think that if it's good, then more is better. This is especially true with sensitive animals: they are entrusting us to use essential oils safely and wisely. Always use the rule 'when in doubt …don't.'
- When using essential oils within a barn or kennel type facility it is best to store aromatherapy products in aroma-safe containers and in a locked cabinet.
- Be mindful of your fellow barn/stable/kennel mates and their animal friends. Remember that not everyone can tolerate the same aromas that you and your animals enjoy. Smell is unique to each individual and lavender is not loved by all!

You can get more information about safety, essential oils and your dog from the following resources:

Natural Dog Health Remedies at www.natural-dog-health-remedies.com

Dogs Naturally Magazine at www.dogsnaturallymagazine.com

Experience Essential Oils at www.experience-essential-oils.com/home-remedies-for-dogs.html

BEST APPLICATION TECHNIQUES

So now that we've looked at safety, it's time to talk about proper application for essential oils. As the chart below demonstrates, there are many ways to do that, it just depends on the oil. Later on in this book, a chapter will go into much more detail about the relevant essential oils and how each one should be administered.

How to use Essential Oils with Pets

- Diffusing – Ensure your animal is able to move away from the diffuser it they do not like it.
- Petting – Take 1 drop of oil in your hands, rub them together until no residue is left on your palm & pet your animal. Avoid the sensitive areas of their face, nose, or the bottoms of their feet.
- Internally – Start with 1 drop in their water or food. You can mix with NingXia Red, coconut oil, honey or red agave.
- Indirect – Place 1 drop in your palm, rub in, and then rub onto something your pet can approach (bedding or the perch of a bird cage).
- Water Misting – Add 4 oz. of water and 1 drop of oil into a glass spray bottle. Shake well & then mist.
- Oil Misting – Mix an oil with a carrier oil in a glass spray bottler & spray your pet. (1:4 ratio)
- Topically – Allow 1 drop of oil to drip right onto the animal
- Raindrop – Similar to the human raindrop technic were you drip oils along the spine from tail to head

Remember your pets will pick up on your energy – maintain a positive attitude when applying oils.

Below is a general guide for *application techniques*:

Aromatically – For dogs, essential oils can be used aromatically by putting a drop of the essential oil on their collar or on their dog bed. You can also make a spray by adding a few essential oil drops to water and spraying the dog's fur.

Topically – You can apply essential oils to the spine, ears, or even on the toes/pads of dogs. You can apply essential oils directly to the wound pretty much anywhere on the body. But remember to *avoid* the eyes, nose, anal and genital areas.

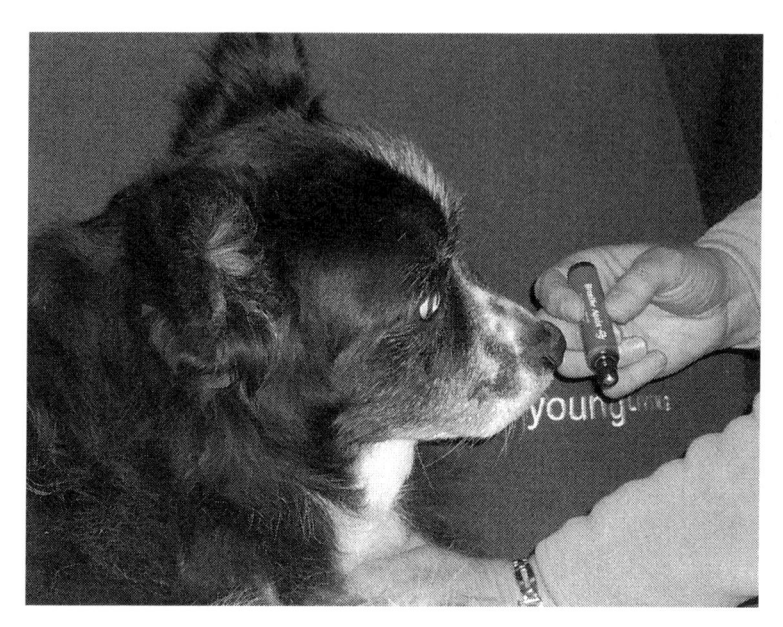

Canine Reflexology Chart

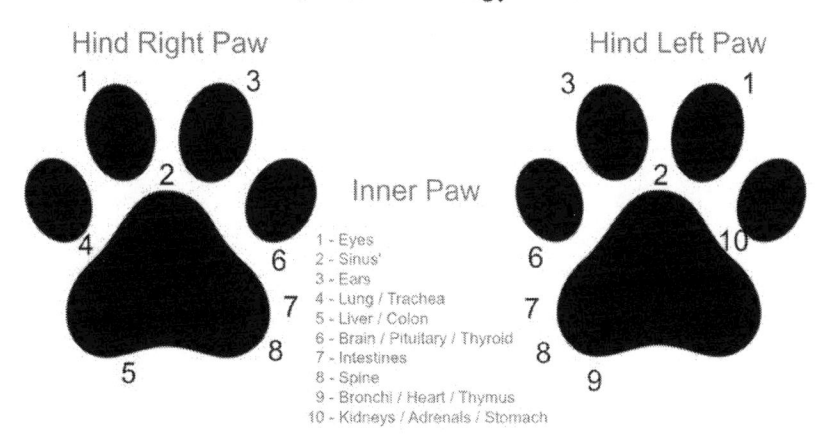

Hind Right Paw

Hind Left Paw

Inner Paw

1 - Eyes
2 - Sinus'
3 - Ears
4 - Lung / Trachea
5 - Liver / Colon
6 - Brain / Pituitary / Thyroid
7 - Intestines
8 - Spine
9 - Bronchi / Heart / Thymus
10 - Kidneys / Adrenals / Stomach

Internally – Before you ingest *any* essential oils or make your pets ingest them, you must understand that they **must be Certified Pure Therapeutic Grade**. You can put the essential oils in an empty gel capsule or in your dog's food if they don't mind the flavor. It is recommended only administering one drop when allowing a dog to ingest internally.

It is also recommended that you should *always* avoid the nose, anal area and genitals when it comes to application. With the use of essential oils on animals, you will have to gauge whether your pet likes the application and reacts well to it.

Remember, no one knows your dog better than you!

5 ULTIMATE STEPS FOR BLENDING ESSENTIAL OILS

When you become confident in the use of essential oils, there may come a time when you want to create your own. There is an entire chapter in this book with recipes for essential oils to help with common dog ailments, so you can give this a go if you choose so.

Here is a great step-by-step guide to blending essential oils:

Step 1 – Finding Essential Oils with the Properties You Need

You can do this with a little bit of research. The Internet is a great way to do this, simply use search terms such as 'energizing essential oils' and you'll find many resourcing letting you know what you need.

Step 2 – Blending Essential Oils Based On Their Categories and Notes

Beginners often struggle with this part, but with a little bit of practice, you will quickly come to grips with what needs to be done. You will need to become familiar with the essential oil categories – a term which is used to help you get a great smell with your blended essential oils. It doesn't have impact on the medicinal or therapeutic purposes, but as smell can have a massive impact on how animals react, it's very useful to know.

Essential oils categories are based on their aromas. Oils from the same categories tend to blend well together, but you can mix and match, as shown below:

- Floral
  (i.e. Lavender, Neroli, Jasmine)
- *Woodsy*
  (i.e. Pine, Cedar)
- *Earthy*
  (i.e. Oakmoss, Vetiver, Patchouli)
- *Herbaceous*
  (i.e. Marjoram, Rosemary, Basil)
- *Minty*
  (i.e. Peppermint, Spearmint)
- *Medicinal/Camphorous*
  (i.e. Eucalyptus, Cajuput, Tea Tree)
- *Spicy*
  (i.e. Nutmeg, Clove, Cinnamon)
- *Oriental*
  (i.e. Ginger, Patchouli)
- *Citrus*
  (i.e. Orange, Lemon, Lime)

There is also a suggestion of which of these **categories blend well together**:

- *Florals* blend well with spicy, citrusy and woodsy oils.
- *Woodsy* oils generally blend well with *all* the categories.
- *Spicy* and *oriental oils* blend well with florals, oriental and citrus oils. Be careful not to overpower the blend with the spicy or oriental oils.
- *Minty oils* blend well with citrus, woodsy, herbaceous and earthy oils.

Another term you will become very familiar with is '***Notes***'. The note of an essential oil is based on how quickly it evaporates. When you put a blend of oils on your skin, it will smell one way, but 3 hours later it may smell another way because some of the oils in your blend have evaporated. These notes are based on the musical scale and are referred to as top notes, middle notes, and base notes.

Perfume 101

top notes	middle notes	base notes
wild orange	geranium	sandalwood
jasmine	lemongrass	frankincense
bergamot	clary sage	patchouli
grapefruit	juniper berry	myrrh
lemon	melissa	ylang ylang
coriander	lavender	cassia
rose	marjoram	cedarwood
lime	rosemary	cinnamon
peppermint	cypress	vetiver
basil	black pepper	ginger

Most times, for beginners, it's recommended that you only *start with three oils*. A top note oil, a middle note oil, and a base note oil. The more comfortable and experienced you get with blending essential oils, the more oils you can add to your blends.

Step 3 – Blending and Testing Essential Oil Blends

Once you've narrowed down your oil choices based on what they're used for (*Step 1*) and then narrowed them down again based on their categories and notes (*Step 2*), you're ready to actually **start blending**.

It's recommended that you only ***start with 10 drops of oil*** total so you can test your essential oil blend without wasting too much of your precious oils, in case you don't care for it later.

Remember, you're only working with your essential oils right now…you are not diluting them with carrier oils yet.

Another thing you may be wondering is how much do you use of each oil. The most commonly used rule to go by when creating an essential oil blend is the *30, 50, 20 rule:*

- 30% of your *top note oil.*
- 50% of your *middle note oil.*
- 20% of your *base note oil.*

This is because when you use your blend, you're going to smell all the oils together first. After a while the top note will have evaporated which will leave you with the middle and base note. As more time goes by your middle note will evaporate leaving you with the base note alone. Smell is very important when using essential oils with dogs, so this is very important.

Step 4 – Letting Your Essential Oil Blend "Rest"

This next step is the easy part. Once you've mixed your oils you need to set your new blend aside and let it rest for 24 - 48 hours. This resting period allows the chemicals and constituents of the different essential oils to mix and meld together, helping them blend better.

Step 5 – Testing Your Blend

This is the last step on blending essential oils. At this point, your oils have just finished their resting period. Now it's time to smell them and see what you think. Also, don't forget to check what your dog thinks – after all, they are the one you are creating the blend for.

Next try **diluting some of your blend** in a carrier oil. Remember to take into consideration your dogs size and age when it comes to the percentage of dilution. Everything that you have learned in the Dilution chapter of this book comes into practice here.

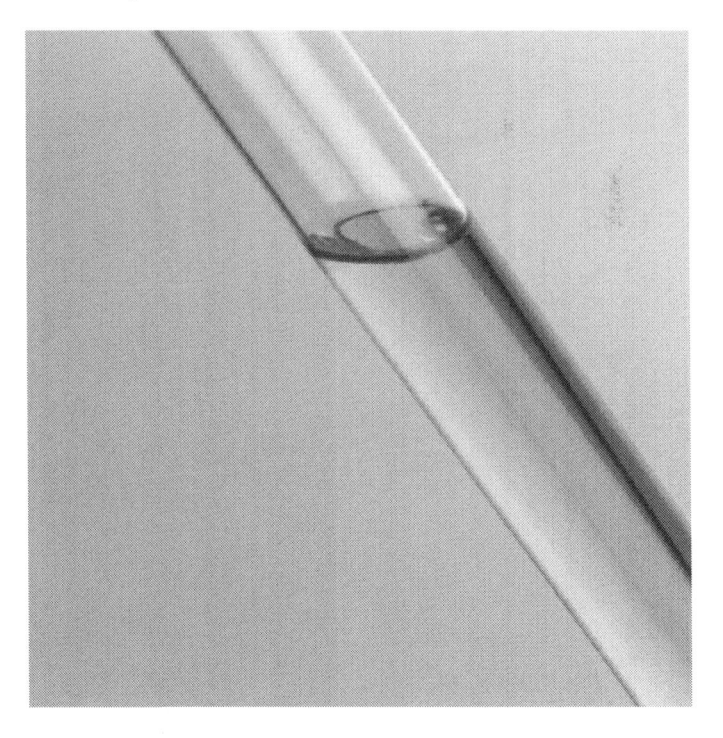

Once you have got the blend right, you can make up more of the oil, allow it to rest then bottle it up to use as necessary. You will get practice with this in the Recipe chapter of this book.

8 TESTED BLENDING TIPS

1. When creating a new blend, start out small with a total number of drops – between 5 and 25. This will ensure that you waste less oil in experiments.
2. Start creating your blend by using *only* essential oils. Wait until you include carrier oils so as not to waste them.
3. Keep a notebook of everything you do, because when the creative juices are flowing you might forget exactly what was written.
4. Perfume sample bottles are great for storage. They're inexpensive and easily found to purchase.
5. Be sure to label your blends clearly. If you don't have to write everything out, but you need some way to decipher what you've created.
6. It is important to use the *30 – 50 – 20 rule* when first starting out blending.
7. Some oils are stronger than others. Unless you *want* certain oils to dominate your blend, it is best to do some research on what you're using. The Internet is filled with online forums and resources which you can use to communicate with others.
8. After creating your blend, it is best to let it sit for a few days before making a decision about whether you love or hate it. The constitutes need time to adjust to one another.

TOP 4 INSIDER TIPS FOR USING ESSENTIAL OILS WITH DOGS

When it comes to using your essential oils with your dog, here are some great tips for you:

WARNING! YOU NEED TO FOLLOW THESE CRUCIAL STEPS BEFORE GIVING YOUR DOG ESSENTIAL OILS!

1. Select essential oils
2. Let your dog smell each bottle, undiluted, lid on
3. Assess your dog's reaction
4. Critical: Let your dog refuse or accept oils!

In the wild, **animals keep themselves healthy by eating plants and minerals that they need**. When your dog eats grass, or drinks from a dirty puddle, he is expressing that instinct. Scientifically this is known as *Zoopharmacognosy*.

When using essential oils, we use this natural sense and allow dogs to select which essential oils and herbal oils they need. In our home, we limit our dogs' choices, controlling what they eat, who they play with, and how they spend their days. This can cause stress, but when we offer essential oils we reduce this stress, by respecting their choices and listening to their preferences. Any time we reduce stress, we increase health.

Zoopharmacognosy: The Basic Rules

First, decide which oils might help your dog. Then, make a shortlist of five or so oils and put the closed bottles on the floor, well-spaced out. Encourage your dog to smell the bottles. Watch carefully and take note of which ones your dog sniffs more intently, or tries to lick. Once he has found the oil he needs, he'll stop sniffing. He might also try to pick up the bottle, so be prepared to stop him from running off with it.

The ability to pick exactly what they need is so acute that researchers have watched dogs go through my collection of 60 essential oils, sniffing the closed bottles, till they find what they want. **Every animal is clear about which essential oil he needs**, and will guide his own healing if given the chance.

The Major Responses

There are three major ways in which dogs choose to interact with aromatic extracts:

1. Smelling
2. Licking
3. Localized topical application

When you offer essential oils to your dog, you must watch carefully, interpret his responses and follow his direction on how he wants to interact with the oils. This develops your listening and observational skills, making you more attentive to your dog in all areas of his life. And your dog loves that.

To start, hold the open bottle in your hand and let your dog come towards it. He may look a little surprised or perplexed at first, sometimes even wary. If your dog likes the oil, he will keep his head turned towards you or come closer. If he does not like the oil, he will turn away, put his head down, or otherwise avoid the smell. Licking the lips quickly is another indication of interest in the oil. A big, yawning lick can indicate they are feeling stressed and you need to move the oil further away.

Allow your dog to settle at a comfortable distance from the bottle; he may move away from it at first. As long as he stays in the room with you, with his nose in your direction, it is a positive response. Allow your dog to leave the area if he chooses. One of the keys to success is patience. Don't rush to decide if your dog likes the oil or not; just wait quietly and give your dog time to decide what he wants to do.

Take the character of each individual into account: shy ones need more time to interact; greedy, enthusiastic types need to settle down and engage fully.

ESSENTIAL OILS TO CONSIDER

So now that you know more about essential oils, you're probably keen to get started using them, so this chapter is going to look at the oils you might like to consider. All of the 30 oils listed below are suitable for dogs and often used in recipes for animal oils.

Top 30 Essential Oils For The Betterment Of Your Dog

1. Lavender

Lavender is an evergreen and fragrant shrub native to southern Europe, especially around the Mediterranean. The majority of the commercial crop is grown in France, Spain, Bulgaria and the Soviet Union. Some is also grown in Tasmania, and there is a minor, but flourishing, industry in Norfolk, England.

Lavender can grow at considerable heights – one organic Provencal grower calls his product '*Lavande 1100*' from the height in metres (3,600 ft) at which his plants are cultivated. Individual lavender plants grow up to 1 m (3 ft) in height, and can become very woody and spreading. The narrow leaves are grey and downy; the flowers are blue-grey, borne on long slender stems. The oil glands are in tiny star-shaped hairs with which the leaves, flowers and stems are covered; rub a flower or leaf between your fingers to release some oil (it has a short-lived aroma).

Distillation method: The straight steam method.

Part of plant used: Flowers, buds and leaves.

Latin name: Lavandula angustifolia.

Color: Clear with a tinge of yellow.

Scent: Floral, fresh, sweet, herbaceous and sometimes fruity.

Uses: Lavender is a soothing and calming oil to help heal sore inflamed areas, burns or wounds. It is often used to deter fleas or to fight allergies.

Application: Aromatic or topically.

Where to buy: Local specialist or online resources, such as Amazon.com, YoungLiving.com, doTerra.com, VioVet.co.uk.

2. Roman Chamomile

Roman Chamomile has daisy-like white flowers and procumbent stems; the leaves are alternate, bipinnate, finely dissected, and downy to glabrous. The solitary, terminal flowerheads, rising 20–30 cm (8–12 in) above the ground, consist of prominent yellow disk flowers and silver-white ray flowers. The flowering time is June and July, and its fragrance is sweet, crisp, fruity and herbaceous.

Distillation method: The straight steam method.

Part of plant used: Flowers.

Latin name: Chamaemelum nobile.

Color: Grey or very pale blue.

Scent: Bright, crisp, sweet, fruity, herbaceous.

Uses: Chamomile is a safe, calming herb that can be used to relieve anxiety, particularly when combined with other herbs. This essential oil has strong anti-inflammatory properties. Can help to sooth sore skin and relieve irritation.

Application: Aromatically or topically.

Where to buy: Local specialist or online resources, such as Amazon.com, YoungLiving.com, NativeAmericanNutritionals.com, HopeWellOils.com.

3. Elemi

Canarium luzonicum, commonly known as elemi, is a tree native to the Philippines. The oleoresin harvested from it is also known as elemi. Elemi resin is a pale yellow substance, of honey-like consistency. Aromatic elemi oil is steam distilled from the resin. It is a fragrant resin with a sharp pine and lemon-like scent. One of the resin components is called *amyrin*.

Elemi resin is chiefly used commercially in varnishes and lacquers, and certain printing inks. It is used as a herbal medicine to treat bronchitis, catarrh, extreme coughing, mature skin, scars, stress, and wounds.

Distillation method: The straight steam method.

Part of plant used: Resin.

Latin name: Canarium luzonicum.

Color: Clear with a tinge of yellow.

Scent: Fresh, citrusy, peppery, spicy.

Uses: Elemi is anti-infectious, antiseptic and works as a sedative. It can be applied topically, orally or it can be diffused.

Application: Aromatically or topically.

Where to buy: Local specialist or online resources, such as Amazon.com, YoungLiving.com, EdensGarden.com, HopeWellOils.com.

4. Myrrh

Myrrh is the aromatic resin of a number of small, thorny tree species of the genus Commiphora, which is an essential oil termed an oleoresin. Myrrh resin is a natural gum. It has been used throughout history as a perfume, incense and medicine. It can also be ingested by mixing it with wine.

When a tree wound penetrates through the bark and into the sapwood, the tree bleeds a resin. Myrrh gum, like frankincense, is such a resin. When people harvest myrrh, they wound the trees repeatedly to bleed them of the gum. Myrrh gum is waxy, and coagulates quickly. After the harvest, the gum becomes hard and glossy. The gum is yellowish, and may be either clear or opaque. It darkens deeply as it ages, and white streaks emerge.

Distillation method: The straight steam method.

Part of plant used: Resin.

Latin name: Commiphora Molmol.

Color: Gold yellow or brown.

Scent: Warm, earthy, woody, balsamic.

Uses: This oil is anti-infectious, anti-inflammatory, antiseptic and also has astringent properties.

Application: Topically.

Where to buy: Local specialist or online resources, such as Amazon.com, YoungLiving.com, MountainRoseHerbs.com, EdensGarden.com.

5. Peppermint

Peppermint is a hybrid mint, a cross between watermint and spearmint. The plant, indigenous to Europe and the Middle East, is now widespread in cultivation in many regions of the world. It is found wild occasionally with its parent species. Peppermint typically occurs in moist habitats, including stream sides and drainage ditches. Being a hybrid, it is usually sterile, producing no seeds and reproducing only vegetatively, spreading by its rhizomes. If placed, it can grow anywhere, with a few exceptions.

Outside of its native range, areas where peppermint was formerly grown for oil often have an abundance of feral plants, and it is considered invasive in Australia, the Galápagos Islands, New Zealand, and in the United States in the Great Lakes region, noted since 1843.

Distillation method: The straight steam method.

Part of plant used: Ariel parts.

Latin name: Mentha piperita.

Color: Clear with a yellow tinge.

Scent: Strong, minty.

Uses: Peppermint is used to ease flatulence, colic and ease digestion. The essential oil in peppermint soothes the stomach lining to help with vomiting and nausea. Can also be used to prevent travel sickness in dogs or to fight asthma and bronchitis.

Application: Aromatically or topically.

Where to buy: Local specialist or online resources, such as Amazon.com, YoungLiving.com, iHerb.com, MountainRoseHerbs.com.

6. Lemon

A lemon is a small evergreen tree native to Asia. The tree's ellipsoidal yellow fruit is used for culinary and non-culinary purposes throughout the world, primarily for its juice, though the pulp and rind (zest) are also used in cooking and baking. The juice of the lemon is about 5% to 6% citric acid, giving the fruit its distinctive, sour taste and making it a key ingredient in drinks and foods such as lemonade and lemon meringue pie.

Distillation method: Cold pressed.

Part of plant used: Peel.

Latin name: Citrus limon.

Color: Pale to dark yellow.

Scent: Fresh concentrated lemon.

Uses: Lemon when applied topically can be used to repel insects and parasites. Mosquitoes do not like the scent of citrus. It can be also used to prevent anxiety, boost the immune and fight infections for your dog.

Application: Topically.

Where to buy: Local specialist or online resources, such as Amazon.com, YoungLiving.com, iHerb.com, HopeWellOils.com.

7. Immortelle (Helichrysum)

Produced in the Mediterranean countries, Madagascar and France this warm, earthy, rich oil is distilled from the flowers. Known for its anti-inflammatory, analgesic and regenerative properties, this remarkable oil is used in many healing formulas from infection and inflammation in respiratory conditions, muscle pain, arthritis to liver problems and as a detoxifier in drug withdrawal.

Distillation method: The straight steam method.

Part of plant used: Flowers.

Latin name: Xerochrysum bracteatum.

Color: Light yellow.

Scent: Fresh, earthy, herbaceous.

Uses: Primarily used for anxiety, bleeding, inflammation, nerve damage, scarring, tumors, and wound care.

Application: Aromatically or topically.

Where to buy: Local specialist or online resources, such as NativeAmericanNutritions.com MountainRoseHerbs.com, EdensGarden.com.

8. Oregano

Oregano oil is derived from the leaves and flowers of oregano, a hardy, bushy perennial herb, and a member of the mint (*Lamiaceae*) family. It's native to Europe, although it grows in many areas around the world. The plant grows up to 90 centimeters (35 inches) high, with dark green leaves that are two to three centimeters long.

The ancient Greeks and Romans have a profound appreciation for oregano, using it for various medicinal uses. In fact, its name comes from the Greek words "oros" and "ganos," which are words for mountain and joy, oregano literally means "joy of the mountain". It was revered as a symbol of happiness, and it was an ancient tradition to crown brides and grooms with a laurel of oregano.

Distillation method: The straight steam method.

Part of plant used: Leaves, flowers and buds.

Latin name: Origanum vulgare.

Color: Pale yellow.

Scent: Herbaceous, sharp.

Uses: Mainly used for the influenza virus, fighting infections and prevent worms.

Application: Topically or internally.

Where to buy: Local specialist or online resources, such as Amazon.com, iHerb.com, YoungLiving.com, MountainRoseHerbs.com.

9. Fennel

The benefits of fennel date back to the ancient Egyptians and Romans. They used fennel for spiritual and emotional support as well as medicinal reasons. Traditionally they used it for snake bites, lung and kidney support and to balance the female reproductive system. Spiritually warriors believed that it gave them courage and strength in battle and longevity. During the Medieval Age, fennel was used to block spells and ward off witches and evil spirits.

Today, we can reap the benefits of fennel using fennel essential oil every day. It can assist us with any kinds of occasional digestive upset. It also is supportive of the circulatory glandular and respiratory systems.

Distillation method: The straight steam method.

Part of plant used: Seeds.

Latin name: Foeniculum vulgare.

Color: Clear with a faint yellow tinge.

Scent: Sweet, spicy, like licorice.

Uses: Fennel assists the adrenal cortex, helps break up toxins and fluid in tissue. It's often used to balance the pituitary, thyroid and pineal glands.

Application: Topically or internally.

Where to buy: Local specialist or online resources, such as Amazon.com, YoungLiving.com, MountainRoseHerbs.com.

10. Spearmint

The use of spearmint oil dates back to ancient times. This perennial herb originated from the Mediterranean region. In Ayurvedic medicine, it was used to treat digestive conditions, skin problems, and headaches. The historical record shows that it was used extensively ancient Greece. It was added to baths and used to treat sexually transmitted diseases, whiten teeth, and heal mouth sores.

In modern times, this essential oil is still widely used as a cure for digestive discomfort, as well as for menstrual problems and nausea.

Distillation method: The straight steam method.

Part of plant used: Leaves, flowers and buds.

Latin name: Mentha spicata.

Color: Clear.

Scent: Minty and slightly fruity.

Uses: Good for colic, diarrhea, nausea. Helps balance metabolism and stimulates the gallbladder.

Application: Aromatically or topically.

Where to buy: Local specialist or online resources, such as Amazon.com, iHerb.com, YoungLiving.com, NowFoods.com.

11. Melissa

Lemon Balm (or Melissa) uses include supportive of immune system function. It is strengthening and revitalizing, yet soothing and calming making it good to ease stress. Several studies report that Melissa may benefit the skin. Lemon Balm has several common names including Sweet Balm and Melissa.

Distillation method: The straight steam method.

Part of plant used: Leaves, flowers and buds.

Latin name: Melissa officinalis.

Color: Yellow.

Scent: Fresh, lemony, herbaceous.

Uses: Melissa is a calming herb that soothes and relaxes. It's also a digestive aid that neutralizes gas in the stomach and intestines. It is also used for muscle-relaxing, fighting flu and immune boost, deodorizing, disinfecting, and insect-repelling benefits.

Application: Aromatically or topically.

Where to buy: Local specialist or online resources, such as Amazon.com, NativeAmericanNutritionals.com, YoungLiving.com, EdensGarden.com.

12. Frankincense

Frankincense, also known as *olibanum*, comes from the *Boswellia* genustrees, particularly *Boswellia sacra* and *Boswellia carteri*. The milky white sap is extracted from the tree bark, allowed to harden into a gum resin for several days, and then scraped off in tear-shaped droplets.

Boswellia trees grow in African and Arabian regions, including Yemen, Oman, Somalia, and Ethiopia. Oman is the best known and most ancient source of frankincense, where it's been traded and shipped to other places like the Mediterranean, India, and China for thousands of years.

Distillation method: The straight steam method.

Part of plant used: Resin.

Latin name: Boswellia.

Color: Light yellow.

Scent: Fresh, woody, balsamic, mildly spicy, fruity.

Uses: Frankincense has been used to help some cases of cancer. It works on the immune system, reduces tumors, inflammations and external ulcers. It can also help fight anxiety, colitis, warts and relief insect/snake bites for your dog.

Application: Topically.

Where to buy: Local specialist or online resources, such as Amazon.com, iHerb.com, YoungLiving.com, NativeAmericanNutritionals.com.

13. Yuzu

Citrus junos is a small tree that produces yellow-golden coloured citrus fruits resembling small oranges or tangerines. The peel of the fruit produces a delightful citrus fragrance with a floral overtone which is quite unique and difficult to describe. This fruit is known in Japan as Yuzu, and like most citrus fruits will yield an essential oil by cold expression.

Distillation method: The straight steam or cold pressed method.

Part of plant used: Peel.

Latin name: Citrus junos.

Color: Greenish orange.

Scent: Bright, complex, citrusy.

Uses: Best used for stomach problems, relaxation and spasms.

Application: Internally.

Where to buy: Local specialist or online resources, such as Amazon.com.

14. Rosemary

Related to mint and looking like lavender, rosemary has leaves like flat pine needles touched with silver. It boasts of a woodsy, citrus-like fragrance that has become a feature of many kitchens, gardens, and apothecaries worldwide. It derives its name from Latin words *ros* ("dew") and *marinus* ("sea"), or "dew of the sea."

The Virgin Mary is said to have spread her blue cloak over a rosemary bush as she rested, and the white flowers turned blue. The shrub came to be known as the "Rose of Mary." Rosemary was considered sacred by the Egyptians, Hebrews, Greeks, and Romans, and was used in the Middle Ages to ward off evil spirits and protect against the plague.

Distillation method: The straight steam method.

Part of plant used: Leaves, flowers and buds.

Latin name: Rosmarinus officinalis.

Color: Clear.

Scent: Fresh, herbaceous, sweet, slightly medicinal.

Uses: A flea repellant.

Application: Topical or Aromatically.

Where to buy: Local specialist or online resources, such as Amazon.com, iHerb.com, YoungLiving.com, NowFoods.com.

15. Cilantro (Coriander)

The health benefits of Coriander Essential Oil can be attributed to its properties as an analgesic, aphrodisiac, antispasmodic, carminative, depurative, deodorant, digestive, fungicidal, lipolytic, stimulant and stomachic substance.

Coriander essential oil is extracted from the seeds of coriander with the help of steam distillation. The scientific name of Coriander is *Coriandrum Sativum*. Coriander essential oil consists of compounds like Borneol, Cineole, Cymene, Dipentene, Linalool, Phellandrene, Pinene, Terpineol and Terpinolene, and these are the causes behind its medicinal properties.

Distillation method: The straight steam method.

Part of plant used: Seeds.

Latin name: Coriandrum sativum.

Color: Pale yellow.

Scent: Sweet, herbaceous, woody, spicy, slightly fruity.

Uses: Mainly used to support digestive health, emotional balance, the nervous system, and immunity.

Application: Topically and internally.

Where to buy: Local specialist or online resources, such as Amazon.com, iHerb.com, YoungLiving.com, MountainRoseHerbs.com.

16 Arborvitae

Known as the "tree of life," Arborvitae is majestic in size and abundant in therapeutic benefits. These trees can be thousands of years old, be dead and lying on the ground but still not be deteriorated at all. Arborvitae essential oil has a high content of tropolones, a group of chemical compounds that protect against environmental and seasonal threats, have powerful purifying properties, and promote healthy cell function. Hinokitiol, one of the tropolones in Arborvitae, protects the body from harmful elements while supporting normal cell activity. This compound also contributes to Arborvitae's natural insect repellent properties. Thujic acid, another tropolone found in Arborvitae, has been studied for its ability to protect against common threats in the environment. Native to Canada, all parts of the Arborvitae tree were used extensively by Native Americans for health benefits and for building vessels, totem poles, baskets, and clothing. Because of its natural preserving properties, Arborvitae prevents wood from rotting, which makes it popular in woodcraft and for preserving natural wood surfaces.

Distillation method: The straight steam method.

Part of plant used: Needles and twigs.

Latin name: Thuja.

Color: Clear to pale yellow/green.

Scent: Pungent, woody, warm.

Uses: Antibacterial, antifungal, antiseptic, anticancer, antitumor, astringent, expectorant, insect repellent, stimulant.

Application: Aromatically or topically.

Where to buy: Local specialist or online resources, such as Amazon.com, EdensGarden.com.

17. Sandalwood

The health benefits of Sandalwood essential oil can be attributed to its properties as an antiseptic, anti-inflammatory, antiphlogistic, antispasmodic, astringent, cicatrisant, carminative, diuretic, disinfectant, emollient, expectorant, hypotensive, memory booster, sedative and tonic substance.

The essential oil of sandalwood is extracted through steam distillation of pieces of wood from matured Sandalwood trees which are 40-80 years old, although 80 years is preferred. The older the tree, the more oil is available, and the aroma is stronger.

Distillation method: The straight steam method.

Part of plant used: Wood.

Latin name: Santalum album.

Color: Clear to pale yellow.

Scent: Rich, sweet, fragrant, woody, floral.

Uses: Mostly used for occasional sleeplessness, digestive imbalance, and regeneration.

Application: Aromatically or topically.

Where to buy: Local specialist or online resources, such as Amazon.com, iHerb.com, YoungLiving.com, MountainRoseHerbs.com.

18. Thyme

Oil of thyme is derived from thyme, also known as *Thymus vulgaris*. The perennial herb, a member of the mint family, is used in aromatherapy, cooking, potpourri, mouthwashes, and elixirs, as well as added to ointments. Thyme also has a number of medicinal properties, which is due to the herb's essential oils.

The benefits of thyme essential oil have been recognized for thousands of years in Mediterranean countries. This substance is also a common agent in Ayurverdic practice. Today, among the many producers of thyme oil, France, Morocco, and Spain emerge as the primary ones.

Distillation method: The straight steam method.

Part of plant used: Leaves, flowers and buds.

Latin name: Thymus vulgaris.

Color: Reddish brown.

Scent: Fresh, medicinal, herbaceous.

Uses: Thyme is a natural antiseptic which is good for digestive problems such as diarrhea, stomach problems, flatulence and poor appetite.

Application: Aromatically, topically or internally.

Where to buy: Local specialist or online resources, such as Amazon.com, iHerb.com, YoungLiving.com, EdensGarden.com.

19. Juniper

The health benefits of Juniper Essential Oil can be attributed to its properties as an antiseptic, sudorific, antirheumatic, depurative, antispasmodic, stimulating, stomachic, astringent, carminative, diuretic, rubefacient, vulnerary and tonic substance.

The essential oil of juniper is obtained through steam distillation of the needles, wood and powdered fruits of juniper, bearing the scientific name *Juniperus Communis*. Its main components are Alpha Pinene, Camphene, Beta Pinene, Sabinene, Myrcene, Alpha Phellandrene, Alpha Terpinene, Gamma Terpinene, Cineole, Beta Phellandrene, Para Cymene, Terpineol, Bornyl Acetate and Caryophyllene and trace amounts of Limonene, Camphor, Linalool, Linalyl Acetate, Borneol and Nerol.

Distillation method: The straight steam method.

Part of plant used: Berries.

Latin name: Juniperus erythrocarpa.

Color: Clear.

Scent: Crisp, woody, sweet, earthy with a slight fruity note.

Uses: Cold, flu, hemorrhoids and obesity.

Application: Internally.

Where to buy: Local specialist or online resources, such as Amazon.com, iHerb.com, YoungLiving.com, MountainRoseHerbs.com.

20. Cardamom

Cardamom (*Elettaria cardamomum*) is a perennial herb that is cultivated in south India and Sri Lanka. The plant belongs to the same family as ginger, and shares the same "warming" properties of the aromatic root. Cardamom was one of the major spices traded between civilizations, and the herb traveled via the Middle East to Ancient Egypt, Greece and Rome. Today, it is widely used in Asian, North African and Middle Eastern cuisines, and its medicinal properties have been mentioned in ancient Vedic texts, which date back to 3000 years! While the Egyptians used cardamom in perfumes and incense, Dioscorides, the Greek physician, pharmacologist, and botanist, described its use in the treatment of sciatica, coughs, spasm, abdominal pains and the retention of urine. In India, cardamom is traditionally used as a digestive aid, as a spice added to food, and on its own as a medicament. However, its most widespread – and by far most interesting – use is as that of an aphrodisiac.

Distillation method: The straight steam method.

Part of plant used: Seeds.

Latin name: Cardamomum.

Color: Clear.

Scent: Spicy, woody, rich, sweet.

Uses: Cardamom is known for its digestive properties. Its warming action strengthens the stomach, spleen and pancreas.

Application: Aromatically or internally.

Where to buy: Local specialist or online resources, such as Amazon.com, iHerb.com, YoungLiving.com, NativeAmericanNutritionals.com.

21. Geranium

The health benefits of Geranium Essential Oil can be attributed to its properties as an astringent, hemostatic, cicatrisant, cytophylactic, diuretic, deodorant, styptic, tonic, vermifuge and vulnerary agent. It is widely used as an element in aromatherapy for its many health benefits, including its ability to balance hormones, relieve stress and depression, reduce inflammation and irritation, improve the health of the skin, alleviate the effects of menopause, improve circulation, benefit dental health, boost kidney health, and reduce blood pressure.

Distillation method: The straight steam method.

Part of plant used: Leaves.

Latin name: Pelargonium.

Color: Ranges from clear to amber.

Scent: Floral, fresh, sweet, slightly fruity.

Uses: Supports healthy circulatory and nervous systems, and has the ability to revitalize body tissues.

Application: Aromatically, topically or internally.

Where to buy: Local specialist or online resources, such as Amazon.com, iHerb.com, YoungLiving.com, HopeWellOils.com.

22. Ginger

Warm, spicy, and energizing, ginger oil comes from ginger root (*Zingiber officinale*), a pungent, peculiar-looking underground rhizome. A member of the Zingiberaceae plant family, this perennial herb grows up to three to four feet high, with narrow spear-shaped leaves, white or yellow flowers, and small tuberous rhizomes with a thick or thin brown skin. Its flesh can be yellow, white, or red, depending on the variety.

Ginger has been valued for thousands of years for its medicinal and culinary properties, particularly in ancient Chinese, Indian, and Greek civilizations. The *Mahabharata*, a 4th century BC Indian Sanskrit epic, even describes a stewed meat dish that uses ginger as an ingredient. In Ayurvedic medicine, ginger is considered a key plant.

Distillation method: The straight steam method.

Part of plant used: Roots.

Latin name: Zingiber officinale.

Color: Light yellow.

Scent: Warm, spicy, earthy, woody.

Uses: Ginger acts on the stomach promoting the flow of gastric juices and thereby assisting the digestion. It also eases problems due to excess acid, flatulence and colic. Ginger is well known for easing travel sickness.

Application: Internally.

Where to buy: Local specialist or online resources, such as Amazon.com, iHerb.com, YoungLiving.com, MountainRoseHerbs.com.

23. Marjoram

The health benefits of Marjoram Essential Oil can be attributed to its properties as an analgesic, antispasmodic, anaphrodisiac, antiseptic, antiviral, bactericidal, carminative, cephalic, cordial, diaphoretic, digestive, diuretic, emenagogue, expectorant, fungicidal, hypotensive, laxative, nervine, sedative, stomachic, vasodilator and vulnerary substance.

This essential oil is extracted by steam distillation of both fresh and dried leaves of the marjoram plant, also known as Knotted Marjoram, which has the scientific name Origanum Marjorana. The main components of marjoram oil are Sabinene, Alpha Terpinene, Gamma Terpinene, Cymene, Terpinolene, Linalool, Sabinene Hydrate, Linalyl Acetate, Terpineol and Gamma Terpineol. This is a plant of the Mediterranean region that has been well known and respected for its medicinal uses for many years.

Distillation method: The straight steam method.

Part of plant used: Leaves, flowers and buds.

Latin name: Origanum majorana.

Color: Clear with a tinge of yellow.

Scent: Herbaceous, sweet, woody with a slight medicinal smell.

Uses: Anti-bacterial, anti-carcinogen, anti-fungal, anti-inflammatory, antioxidant, anti-septic and anti-spasmodic.

Application: Aromatically or topically.

Where to buy: Local specialist or online resources, such as Amazon.com, iHerb.com, YoungLiving.com, HopeWellOils.com.

24. Niaouli

The health benefits of Niaouli Essential Oil can be attributed to its properties as an analgesic, anti-rheumatic, antiseptic, bactericidal, balsamic, cicatrisant, decongestant, expectorant, febrifuge, insecticide, stimulant, vermifuge and vulnerary substance.

Niaouli is a large evergreen tree with the botanical name of Melaleuca Viridiflora and it is a native to Australia and a few neighboring areas. Due to its disinfectant and antiseptic properties, it is widely used in a large variety of cosmetics such as lotions, creams, soaps, and toothpastes.

Distillation method: The straight steam method.

Part of plant used: Leaves.

Latin name: Melaleuca quinquenervia.

Color: Clear.

Scent: Earthy, musty, harsh.

Uses: Mostly used as analgesic, anti-rheumatic, antiseptic, bactericidal, balsamic, cicatrisant, decongestant, expectorant, febrifuge, insecticide, stimulant, vermifuge and vulnerary substance.

Application: Topically.

Where to buy: Local specialist or online resources, such as Amazon.com, EdensGarden.com, YoungLiving.com, NativeAmericanNutritional.com.

25. Sweet Orange

The health benefits of Orange Essential Oil can be attributed to its properties as an anti-inflammatory, antidepressant, antispasmodic, antiseptic, aphrodisiac, carminative, diuretic, tonic, sedative and cholagogue substance.

The essential oil of orange has a wide variety of domestic, industrial and medicinal uses. Domestically, it is used to add orange flavor to beverages, desserts and sweetmeats. Industrially, it is used in soaps, body lotions, creams, anti-aging and wrinkle-lifting applications, concentrates for soft beverages, room fresheners, sprays, deodorants, biscuits, chocolates, confectionery and bakery items.

Distillation method: Cold pressed.

Part of plant used: Peel.

Latin name: Citrus sinensi.

Color: Greenish orange.

Scent: Citrusy and sweet.

Uses: Calming, deodorizing, flea-repelling. Caution: Can cause photosensitization. Avoid the sun after use.

Application: Aromatically or topically.

Where to buy: Local specialist or online resources, such as Amazon.com, iHerb.com, YoungLiving.com, MountainRoseHerbs.com.

26. Vetiver

Chrysopogon zizanioides, commonly known as *vetiver*, is a perennial grass that belongs to the Poaceae family, which is native to India. Western and Northern India know this plant as khus. Vetiver (Vetiveria zizanioides), derived from a Tamil word that means "hatcheted up," can grow up to 1.5 meters, and have tall stems and long, thin, and rigid leaves. Its flowers are brownish-purple. Vetiver hails from India but is widely cultivated in the world's tropical regions.

Vetiver essential oil is derived through the steam distillation of the plant's roots. It has a strong initial aroma and is described as woody, smokey, earthy, herbaceous, and spicy. While not widely known, it dates back centuries and, in the 12th century, even became a taxable item in India. Perhaps the most valued quality of vetiver oil is that it is deeply grounding, and often used for promoting sleep. It is said to also be equally helpful for restlessness.

Distillation method: The straight steam method.

Part of plant used: Root.

Latin name: Chrysopogon zizanioides.

Color: Golden to dark brown.

Scent: Woody, earthy, smoky, herbaceous, spicy.

Uses: Vetiver is very grounding and calming. It also has been documented to relieve shock and trauma.

Application: Aromatically.

Where to buy: Local specialist or online resources, such as Amazon.com, YoungLiving.com, doTerra.com, iHerb.com.

27. Bergamot

The health benefits of Bergamot Essential Oil can be attributed to its properties as a deodorant, vulnerary, vermifuge, antibiotic, antiseptic, antispasmodic, sedative, analgesic, antidepressant, disinfectant, febrifuge, cicatrisant, and digestive substance.

Bergamot is a citrus fruit whose rind is used for extracting the Bergamot Essential Oil. The scientific name of bergamot is *Citrus Aurantium var.* or *Citrus Bergamia*. It is a tropical plant, but thrives in Europe as well. Its powerful aroma makes it a popular component in many perfumes, and it is often used as the all-important "top note". It is derived through cold compression, opposed to the steam distillation of many other essential oils. One of the most common applications that you may not be aware of is its use in black tea. The inclusion of bergamot essential oil in regular black tea is then given a different name – Earl Grey!

Distillation method: Cold pressed.

Part of plant used: Peel.

Latin name: Citrus bergamia.

Color: Green or golden.

Scent: Fresh, citrusy, slightly floral.

Uses: Mainly an antifungal, used for its soothing properties. Excellent for ear infections.

Application: Topical.

Where to buy: Local specialist or online resources, such as Amazon.com, YoungLiving.com, MountainRoseHerbs.com, iHerb.com.

28. Carrot Seed

The health benefits of carrot seed essential oil can be attributed to its properties as an antiseptic, disinfectant, detoxifying, antioxidant, anticarcinogenic, carminative, depurative, diuretic, emenagogue, stimulant, cytophylactic, tonic, and vermifuge substance.

Carrot seed essential oil, as the name suggests, is extracted by steam distillation, primarily from the dried seeds of wild carrot, but also from the dried plant itself. Its scientific name is *Daucus Carota*, and the wild carrot is common in Europe, though it is often known by another name in that region, which is "Queen Anne's Lace".

Distillation method: The straight steam method.

Part of plant used: Seeds.

Latin name: Daucus carota.

Color: Golden yellow.

Scent: Earthy, woody, warm, harsh.

Uses: Mainly used for its anti-inflammatory properties, but also has moderate antibacterial effects. Can rejuvenate and stimulate tissue regeneration, thus effective for scar healing.

Application: Topically.

Where to buy: Local specialist or online resources, such as Amazon.com, YoungLiving.com, HopeWellOils.com, iHerb.com.

29. Cedarwood

Cedar oil, also known as Cedarwood oil, is an essential oil derived from the foliage, and sometimes the wood and roots, of various types of conifers, most in the pine or cypress botanical families. It has many uses in medicine, art, industry and perfumery, and while the characteristics of oils derived from various species may themselves vary, all have some degree of bactericidal and pesticidal effects.

Although termed cedar or cedarwood oils, the most important oils of this group are produced from distilling wood of a number of different junipers and cypresses (Juniperus and Cupressus spp., of the family Cupressaceae), rather than true cedars (Cedrus spp., of the family Pinaceae). A cedar leaf oil is also commercially distilled from the Eastern arborvitae (Thuja occidentalis, also of the Cupressaceae), and similar oils are distilled, pressed or chemically extracted in small quantities from wood, roots and leaves from plants of the genera Platycladus, Cupressus, Taiwania and Calocedrus.

Distillation method: The straight steam method.

Part of plant used: Wood.

Latin name: Cedrus atlantica.

Color: Light to golden yellow.

Scent: Woody, sweet.

Uses: Cedarwood is an oil which contains antiseptic and anti-fungal properties.

Application: Aromatically.

Where to buy: Local specialist or online resources, such as Amazon.com, YoungLiving.com, doTerra.com, iHerb.com.

30. Eucalyptus

The health benefits of eucalyptus oil are well-known and wide ranging, and its properties include anti-inflammatory, antispasmodic, decongestant, deodorant, antiseptic, antibacterial, stimulating, and other medicinal qualities. Eucalyptus essential oil is colorless and has a distinctive taste and odor.

Though eucalyptus essential oil has most of the properties of a typical volatile oil, it's not very popular as an aromatherapy oil because little was known about it until recent centuries, rather than the more ancient aromatherapy substances. The numerous health benefits of eucalyptus oil have attracted the attention of the entire world, and it has stimulated a great deal of exploration into its usage in aromatherapy as well as in conventional medicine.

Distillation method: The straight steam method.

Part of plant used: Leaves.

Latin name: Eucalyptus Radiata.

Color: Clear.

Scent: Fresh, medicinal, earthy, woody.

Uses: Antiviral, anti-inflammatory, an expectorant. Good for relief of chest congestion. Effective in repelling flea.

Application: Topically.

Where to buy: Local specialist or online resources, such as Amazon.com, YoungLiving.com, EdensGarden.com, iHerb.com.

Of course, there are many essential oils that are very effective for use with dogs; this list is by no means exhaustive. This 30 is just to get you started, a little bit of research will lead you to lots more.

Below are some of the oils for pet care recommended by *Young Living*.

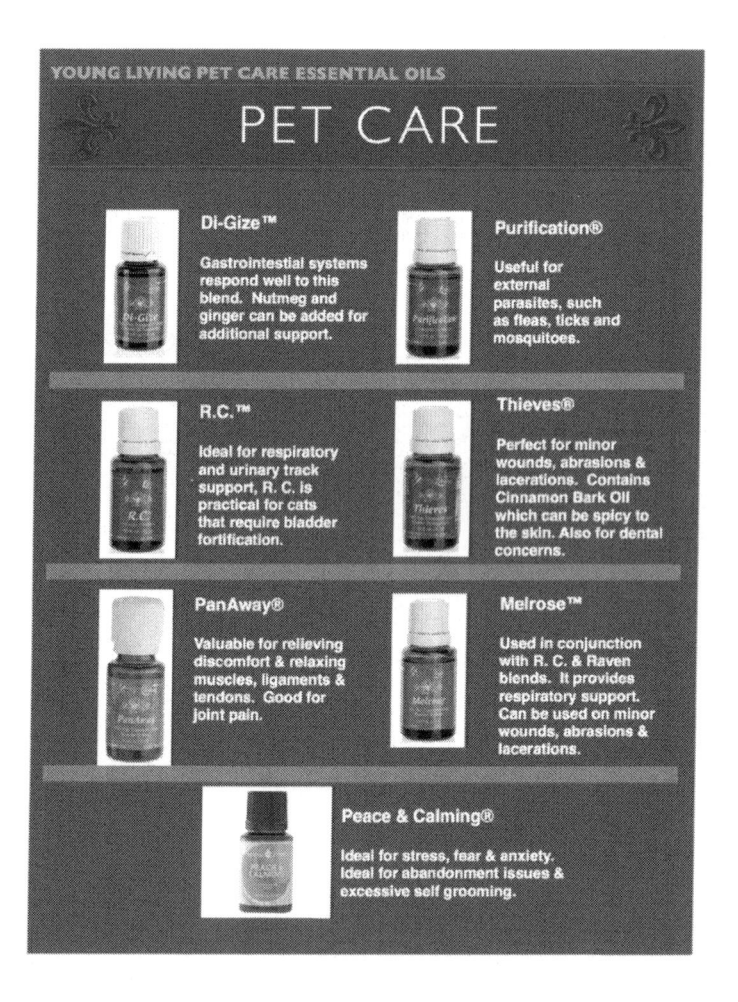

YOUNG LIVING PET CARE ESSENTIAL OILS

PET CARE

Di-Gize™
Gastrointestinal systems respond well to this blend. Nutmeg and ginger can be added for additional support.

Purification®
Useful for external parasites, such as fleas, ticks and mosquitoes.

R.C.™
Ideal for respiratory and urinary track support, R. C. is practical for cats that require bladder fortification.

Thieves®
Perfect for minor wounds, abrasions & lacerations. Contains Cinnamon Bark Oil which can be spicy to the skin. Also for dental concerns.

PanAway®
Valuable for relieving discomfort & relaxing muscles, ligaments & tendons. Good for joint pain.

Melrose™
Used in conjunction with R. C. & Raven blends. It provides respiratory support. Can be used on minor wounds, abrasions & lacerations.

Peace & Calming®
Ideal for stress, fear & anxiety.
Ideal for abandonment issues & excessive self grooming.

Dog Vita Flex Chart

Hind Paw (Right) Hind Paw (Left)

1. Eyes
2. Sinus
3. Ears
4. Lung/Trachea
5. Liver/Colon
6. Brain/Pituitary/Thyroid
7. Intestines
8. Spine
9. Bronchi/Heart/Thymus
10. Kidney/Adrenal/Stomach

Peppermint
Beneficial when used with PanAway on minor injuries for aches and pains. Use 1 drop in water for over heated animals (great on long walks). Cats must have this oil diluted.

Thieves
The ideal solution for treating minor injuries with contamination. Can be used for dental issues. The best oil for immune system support listed here. Safe to use topically or internally. Great for ticks.

Lemon
Beneficial for increasing awareness in training or cognitive issues. Use in combination with other oils safely for protection against parasites. Excellent for skin conditions. Can be used topically or ingested.

Lavender
Ideal for minor injuries. Gentle at cleansing. Add peppermint oil to increase the healing process while decreasing aches and pain. Repels parasites. Calms the nervous system. Aids in skin and tissue health.

Frankincense
A safe and gentle oil that is recommended for smaller pets and birds. Used for wounds, skin health, tissue health, behavior issues, cleansing, fungus and more. One of the best go-to oils.

PanAway
Best oil blend for minor injuries. (Dilute before using on cats) Great for urinary health, aches & pains, dental extraction or minor discomfort. Use topically with a warm compress, or Vita Flex points on the paws

27 RISKY ESSENTIAL OILS TO AVOID FOR YOUR DOG

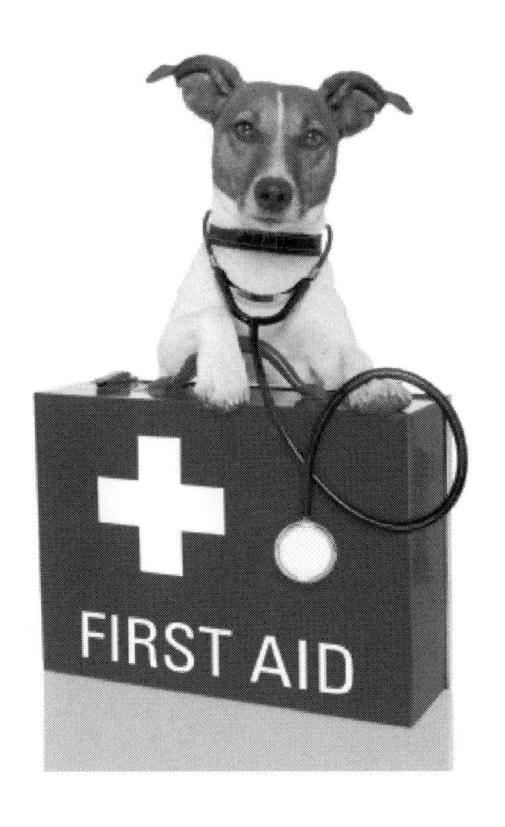

There are a number of essential oils that are advised against when it comes to animals, including dogs. These can have negative effects on your pets that I'm sure you'd prefer to avoid.

Below is a list of **27 oils that *may* be of risk to animals** (not necessarily dogs, so it is best to check with a medical professional before using any of these):

1. Anise (Pimpinella anisum)
2. Birch (Betula)
3. Bitter Almond (Prunus dulcis)
4. Boldo (Peumus boldus)
5. Calamus (Acorus calamus)
6. Camphor (Cinnamomum camphora)
7. Cassia (Cassia fistula)
8. Chenopodium (Chenopodium album)
9. Cloves (Syzygium aromaticum)
10. Garlic (Allium sativum)
11. Goosefoot (Chenopodium murale)
12. Horseradish (Armoracia rusticana)
13. Hyssop (Hyssopus sp. with the exception of Decumbens)
14. Mugwort (Artemisia vulgaris)
15. Mustard (Brassica juncea)
16. Pennyroyal (Mentha pulegium)
17. Rue (Ruta graveolens)
18. Santolina (Santolina chamaecyparissus)
19. Sassafras (Sassafras albidum)
20. Savory (Satureja)
21. Tansy (Tanacetum vulgare)
22. Tea Tree Oil (Melaleuca alternifolia)
23. Terebinth (Pistacia palaestina)
24. Thuja (Thuja occidentalis)
25. Wintergreen (Gaultheria procumbens)
26. Wormwood (Artemisia absinthium)
27. Yarrow (Achillea millefolium)

STEPS TO TAKE IF YOU SUSPECT POISONING

PET POISON HELPLINE
800.213.6680
www.petpoisonhelpline.com

If you're careful and follow the guidelines associated with essential oils, poisoning is *very* unlikely. However, it is best to be well informed in all areas before use, which is why this guide from VCA Hospitals (www.vcahospitals.com) has been included:

"Essential oils contain chemicals that are rapidly absorbed orally or through the skin. Many of these chemicals are metabolized through the liver. Very young dogs and ones with liver disease are more sensitive to their effects.

They can also irritate or burn the skin and mouth. Only a couple of licks or a small amount on the skin could be harmful to a dog, depending on the ingredients in a specific product and how the pet is exposed."

The symptoms of poisoning can be:

- Fragrance or scent on hair, coat, skin, breath or in the vomit.
- Difficulty breathing.
- Difficulty walking or uncoordinated gait.
- Drooling.
- Lethargy or weakness.
- Muscle tremors.
- Pawing at the mouth or face.
- Redness or burns to the lips, gums, tongue or skin.
- Vomiting.

If you believe that your dog has been poisoned by essential oils, you need to contact a medical professional immediately, for example the **Pet Poison Helpline** (www.petpoisonhelpline.com 800-213-6680). **You must also:**

- *Not* induce vomiting or give activated charcoal to your dog as it may worsen their condition.
- Put the product packaging in a sealed plastic bag and take it to the veterinary clinic with you.
- If any product is on the skin or fur, quickly wash it off using hand washing detergent.

Fast and immediate treatment from a veterinarian is necessary if your dog has been poisoned by essential oils. **The medical professional may then do one of a number of things**:

- Perform blood work to determine if the liver and kidneys have been affected.
- Intravenous fluids may be used for hydration.
- Sometimes a soft diet or feeding tube may be needed if there are chemical burns in the mouth or esophagus.
- Medication for vomiting, stomach issues, pain, antibiotics, etc. may be issued.

So try to avoid this, keep products stored out of your dog's reach. It is also within your pets' best interest to consult your vet before using any essential oils, and remember to *never* use concentrated oils on your dog.

40 LITTLE KNOWN ESSENTIAL OIL RECIPES

Now that you know a lot more about the essential oil ingredients that are great for use with dogs, here are some recipes that you can easily make at home for common ailments.

Note that most of recipes require diluting the essential oils with the carrier oil.

The best option for base/carrier oil is organic fractionated coconut oil, cold pressed olive oil, or grape seed oil. Coconut oil spoils the slowest of the carrier oils. Avoid nut oils if your pet is allergic to nuts. You can also use V-6 enhanced vegetable oil complex by Young Living as a carrier oil. Never use water for dilution of essential oil as they do not mix! Water can cause the oil to irritate your pet's skin more.

If any essential oil gets into your pet's eyes, rinse with carrier oil, never use water!

1. Motion Sickness

Car sickness can be difficult when it comes to animals because there are times when we need to take them travelling. This blend is effective in calming the stomach of a dog with motion sickness.

Ingredients:

- 2 oz. (60 ml) base oil (e.g. olive oil, fractionated coconut oil, jojoba oil)

- 7 drops of Ginger Essential Oil
- 5 drops of Peppermint Essential Oil

This recipe is for a medium dog, but can be changed slightly to suit. Dilute using your base oil according to your dog's age and size. (Use the guide in the <u>Dilution</u> chapter in this book for details on how to do this).

Apply the oil blend to the inside tip of the dog's ears, under his "armpit", and on his belly. You can also add a few drops of the oil blend to a cotton ball and put it in the car (in front of the air vent) to circulate the scent in the car.

2. Energy Boost

Prepare the following dog aromatherapy blend by pouring the essential oils into a 10 ml bottle and adding organic vegetable oil to fill. Dilute according to your dog's age and size, this recipe is for a medium dog. Apply by massaging the spine gently and use in the mornings only.

Ingredients:

- 6 drops Lavender
- 5 drops Rosemary
- 2 drops Peppermint

3. Dog Shampoo

This shampoo recipe can be helpful to support the skin and coat, building up your dog's immunity.

Ingredients:

- 1 cup water
- 1 tablespoon of castile soap
- 1/4 tsp vitamin E
- 3 drops of peppermint essential oil
- 3 drops of lavender essential oil
- 2 drops of Roman chamomile
- 2 drops of Purification
- 1 drops of cedar wood
- *optional*: 2 drops of citronella

Mix all of this together in a jar and use straight. This recipe is suitable for a dog of any age, but seek advice if your dog is very young, very old or has sensitive skin. It's watery, but use it like you would normal dog shampoo.

4. Anxiety

This aromatherapy recipe is effective for calming dogs that have separation anxiety, noise anxiety, or fear of new places, people, or things.

Ingredients:

- 2 oz. (60 ml) base oil (e.g. olive oil, fractionated coconut oil, jojoba oil)
- 3-4 drops Valerian
- 3-4 drops Lavender
- 2 drops Clary Sage
- 2 drops Sweet Marjoram

This recipe is suitable for a small to medium sized dog, but can be edited as needed. Dilute according to your dogs age and size.

Use this blend topically on your dog. Rub 2 to 3 drops of the essential oil blend between your hands and apply it on the edge of your dog's ears, between the toes, on his inner thighs, or under his "armpits".

You can also make a lavender powder for dogs who are stressed and have anxiety issues. Baking soda, rice flour, or cornstarch can be used to dilute essential oils, making them safe for dogs.

For this calming lavender powder, you need the following essential oils:

- 3 parts of Lavender
- 2 parts of Bergamot
- 2 parts of Melissa
- 1 part of Ylang Ylang

Use 12 to 15 drops of this essential oil blend per cup of baking soda, or use a blend of baking soda and rice flour. Stir or shake to mix well. Again, you can dilute this according to your dog's size and age.

If your dog is stressed during a car ride to the vet, for example, sprinkle the powder on a blanket and put it inside the cage with the dog. If your dog has separately anxiety while you are not home, sprinkle the powder on an old clothes of yours and put it on your dog's bed. Your smell from your old clothes reassures your dog, and the calming effects of the oil blend may help him relax.

5. Insect Repellent

This great blend will help your dog prevent all type of insects, like ticks, mosquitoes, etc.

Prepare the following blend by pouring the essential oils into a 16 oz. glass spray bottle.

Ingredients:

- 2 cups of water
- 8 drops Lavender
- 8 drops Peppermint

Mist dog everyday avoiding eyes and nose. Spray on bedding or dog clothes as well.

To repel insects, pure Geranium essential oil can also be used. If used alone as a spray, it is suggested that you put no more than 4 drops per half cup of water and keep it refrigerated. Shake before spraying a light spritz on the pets' fur. No need to make the fur all wet, the bugs are repelled from the scent of it. Do not get in the eyes, nose or mouth.

6. Ear Health

This recipe is for your dog's ear health. Mix the following ingredients into 1 table spoon of coconut oil (the amount of coconut oil can be changed to dilute the solution according to your dogs size and age).

Ingredients:

- 5 drops of Lavender
- 5 drops of Melaleuca (or Basil)
- 5 drops of Geranium

After cleaning the ear with a natural cleaner, use a Q-tip to rub the essential oil mixture in the ear (being careful not to put the Q-tip in past where you can see it). Do this twice a day until the ear no longer looks red or swollen.

7. Wound Care

Prepare this oil blend, store in a dark glass bottle and put it in your dog's first aid kit. It comes in handy for minor cuts, scrapes, bruises, insect bites, and other small wounds.

Ingredients:

- 2 oz. (60 ml) base oil (e.g. olive oil, fractionated coconut oil, jojoba oil)
- 5 drops Lavender
- 2 drop Helichrysum
- 2 drops Sweet Marjoram
- 2 drops Niaouli

The base oil amount can be changed to dilute the oil according to your dog's size and age. This remedy is to be applied topically to the injured area using a cotton wool bud and 2 to 3 drops of oil.

8. Insect Bites

This recipe is great for dealing with insect bites on your dog.

Ingredients:

- 2 drops Thyme (Use with caution as it is not recommended for dogs in some cases)
- 10 drops Lavender
- 4 drops Eucalyptus Radiata
- 3 drops German Chamomile
- 20 drops V-6 vegetable oil complex

This recipe is for large dogs (Use the guide in the <u>Dilution</u> chapter in this book for details on how to dilute for your needs). Put all ingredients into dark glass bottle, turn gently to mix. Apply directly to the bite 1 to 2 drops 2 to 4 times daily as needed for relief.

9. Ear Infections

This recipe is for ear issues with dogs. In a 2 ounce glass spray bottle, combine the following ingredients:

- 15 drops Lavender
- 15 drops Geranium
- 15 drops Frankincense
- 15 drops Basil
- 10 drops Arborvitae
- Fractionated Coconut Oil to fill the bottle about 3/4 of the way full

Change the amount of coconut oil added to dilute according to your dogs age and size. This recipe is for large dogs. Shake bottle well before using. Spray on your dog's ear once a week to treat ears that have an ear infection or once a month as a preventative measure in ears that are prone to recurrent ear infections.

If ears are especially inflamed or infected, dilute 2 drops of lavender in 4 drops of fractionated coconut oil on a cotton ball and apply lightly to soothe the inflamed ear area.

10. Arthritis

Here are two arthritis massage oil recipes.

For *the first one*, the *ingredients* you'll need are:

- 2 oz. (60 ml) base oil (e.g. olive oil, fractionated coconut oil, jojoba oil)
- 4 drops Helichrysum
- 2 drops Peppermint
- 2 drops Ginger
- 3 drops Valerian

For *the second one*, you need:

- 2 oz. (60 ml) base oil (e.g. olive oil, fractionated coconut oil, jojoba oil)
- 4 drops Rosemary oil
- 3 drops Lavender
- 4 drops Ginger

Use either of these 2 blends topically to massage your dog's sore joints, or pain caused by arthritis or dysplasia. Put a drop or two on the inside of his ear tips as well. Both of these recipes, which are designed for medium sized dogs, can be changed to suit your dog's age and size using the <u>Dilution</u> guide in this book.

11. Separation Anxiety

This essential oil blend can help your dog deal with separation anxiety.

Ingredients:

- 5 drops Geranium
- 5 drops Ylang Ylang
- 5 drops Roman or Blue Chamomile

Blend with 8 ounces of carrier oil for a small to medium dog (this can be changed to suit your needs by following the <u>Dilution</u> guide) or water in a spray bottle.

Lavender and Roman Chamomile can be used individually for calming.

12. Nausea and Vomiting

This essential oil for nausea is a great way to settle your pet's stomach.

Ingredients:

- 1 table spoon of Sweet Almond oil (for the carrier oil)
- 7 drops Peppermint essential oil.
- 6 drops Ginger essential oil.

Blend well and shake before using. Place one to three drops (based on size – one for a small dog, two medium, three large) on your dog's tongue. If you wish to dilute the oil according to your dog's age, you can change the recipe to suit. You may also place a couple of drops on a cotton pad for aromatherapy. Hold it around the dog's nose or place close to his crate (safely out of reach).

13. Tick Repellent

Ticks hate geranium, bay, and lavender. Here is an oil blend that can keep ticks off your dog.

Ingredients:

- 2 oz. (60 ml) base oil (e.g. olive oil, fractionated coconut oil, jojoba oil)
- 5 drops Lavender
- 4 drops Geranium
- 3 drops Lemon Eucalyptus

Apply a few drops of the oil blend to the neck, back, chest, legs, and tail of your dog. This recipe is for a medium sized dog. If you wish to change the recipe to suit your needs, consult the Dilution chapter of this book.

14. Joint Pain Relief

Pain in the joints is a nightmare for dogs, so this blend can help you with this.

Ingredients:

- 30 drops Idaho Balsam fir
- 10 drops Helichrysum
- 5 drops Peppermint
- 1 drop Oregano (use with caution as this oil is not recommended for dogs in some cases)

Put all ingredients into dark glass bottle, turn gently to mix. Apply 2 to 3 drops of the straight mixture to the affected joint 3 times daily. This recipe is for a large dog (Use the guide in the Dilution chapter in this book for details on how to dilute for your needs).

15. Sunscreen

Mix this blend and put it on your dog's nose to protect it from the sun.

Ingredients:

- 25 drops Carrot Seed oil
- 20 drops Myrrh
- 5 drops Helichrysum
- 2 Tablespoons V-6 or thin carrier oil

This recipe is for a large sized dog. If you wish to change the blend for your dog's age and size, check the <u>Dilution</u> guide in this book.

16. Bad Odor

These recipes are easy to make and your dog will certainly smell fresh and lovely! You can add essential oils to an all natural shampoo to fight bad dog odor.

To 8 oz. (240 ml) of an all natural shampoo, add:

- 4 drops Chamomile Roman
- 4 drops Geranium
- 7-8 drops Lavender
- 3 drops Sweet Marjoram

This recipe will work for dogs of any age and size, but consult a health professional first if your dog is very young, very old or has sensitive skin. This mix is to be used as normal dog shampoo.

On a damp, rainy day, the "doggie smell" from our four-legged friends may be more profound than ever. Use this quick-and-easy spray to get rid of that smell:

To 1 cup of distilled water, add:

- 10 drops Lavender
- 6 drops Sweet Orange
- 6 drops Peppermint

- 3 drops Eucalyptus

Mix well in a spray bottle. This recipe is for a medium sized dog. You can dilute it differently if necessary.

Cover your dog's face and eyes with one hand and spray directly on your dog's body, avoiding the head. You can even spray your room with this blend. This is refreshing and the antibacterial properties of lavender and eucalyptus will sanitize your room as well!

17. Itchiness

This recipe has been used to help with itchiness and it's been very effective in helping to decrease itching and reduce redness.

Ingredients:

- 5 oz of carrier oil such as fractionated coconut oil or olive oil
- 3 drops of vitamin E
- 5 drops of Lavender essential oil
- 5 drops of Roman Chamomile
- 2 to 3 drops of Frankincense (optional)

Mix this together in the glass dropper bottle and apply 2 to 4 drops directly to the spot to help soothe the skin twice a day or as needed for itching. You can also use this for any patches of skin which happen to be dry and need extra moisture. You can edit this recipe, which is for medium sized dogs, to suit your dog's age and size by using the correct amount of carrier oil suggested in the Dilution guide of this book.

18. Pet Powder for fleas

This powder is a great preventative method for fleas.

Ingredients:

- 2 drops Juniper oil
- 2 drops Lavender oil
- 1/2 cup Arrowroot (or cornstarch, clay, baking soda, or equal part blend of these)

Combine the arrowroot and essential oils (changing the amount according to the Dilution guide – the 2 drops are for small to medium sized dogs), crushing the Clumps of oil between your fingers to evenly.

Sprinkle on your pet as a preventive measure. Be sure to wash your hands after handling the pure essential oils to avoid any contact with the eyes or delicate mucous membranes.

19. Skin Problems

You can either add the following recipe to 8 oz. (240 ml) of an all-natural shampoo to make a soothing shampoo or to 1/2 oz. of a base oil to make an oil blend for dog itchy skin. Use the oil blend topically on affected skin areas, as you would a normal dog shampoo. This recipe is for a medium sized dog (Use the guide in the <u>Dilution</u> chapter in this book for details on how to dilute for your needs).

Ingredients:

- 4 drops Lavender
- 2 drops Geranium
- 3 drops German Chamomile
- 3 drops Carrot Seed

20. Diarrhea and Stomach cramps

Diarrhea is a common canine affliction and it varies in frequency, duration, and intensity from dog to dog.

You may not be able to totally prevent diarrhea, but knowing as much as possible about it might help limit the number times your dog has one of these unpleasant episodes and reduce the duration when the runs do come.

Dogs suffering from diarrhea very often have stomach cramps. Antispasmodic oils such as peppermint or chamomile are effective in stopping the cramping.

Ingredients:

- 3 drops Peppermint
- 3 drops Roman Chamomile
- Half a teaspoon of carrier oil (e.g. olive oil, fractionated coconut oil)

Mix all components together and rub the oil mixture on the tips of your dog's ears. This recipe is for a medium sized dog, but can be changed to suit your needs using the Dilution chapter in this book.

Single Peppermint oil is wonderful for treating diarrhea and vomiting. Rub on the bare belly or the gums. Be sure to dilute with the base/carrier oil formula.

21. Relaxation

A blend from doTerra is brilliant for relaxing muscles, calming tension, soothing irritated tissue and increasing circulation. It is called *AromaTouch* and uses the following ingredients:

The essential oils of:

- Basil.
- Grapefruit.
- Cypress.
- Marjoram.
- Peppermint.
- Lavender.

It is applied topically to your dog, massaged into your dog's spine. Mixing using the <u>Dilution</u> guide in this book.

22. Ear Infections

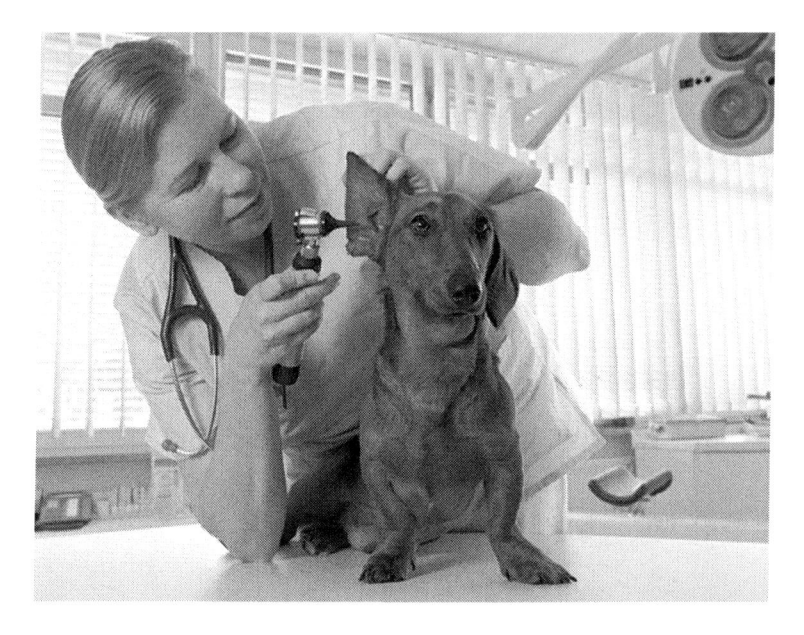

This is one of the most helpful aroma recipes for dogs with long ears! This essential oil recipe is effective in preventing and treating ear infections in dogs, and can be used after you have cleaned out your dog's ears.

Ingredients:

- 2 oz. (60 ml) base oil (e.g. olive oil, fractionated coconut oil, jojoba oil)
- 4 drops Lavender
- 2 drops Niaouli
- 3 drops Bergamot
- 3 drops Roman Chamomile

This recipe is for a medium sized dog, but you can edit the amount of carrier oil used to dilute the recipe according to your dog's size and age. Mix the oils in a dark glass bottle and use a dropper to drip a few drops of the oil blend into your dog's ear canal and gently massage the outside of the ear. Then, clean the ear with a cotton ball. The oil blend loosens and washes out all the dirt in the ear, making it less prone to ear infections. The antibacterial and antiviral properties of lavender and niaouli speed up the healing of an ear infection.

Alternatively, **Purification** is blend of essential oils made by Young Living and is wonderful for cleaning dog's ears. Put a drop of purification on the palm of your hand, rub the end of a Q-tip in the drop then clean your dog's ear. Repeat the process with a fresh end of a Q-tip for the other ear. Repeat daily until the Q-tip is free of debris. It kills ear mites instantly.

23. Skin Irritation

This blend is great for soothing your dog's irritated skin.

Ingredients:

- 3 squirts organic Tamanu oil.
- 1 to 2 drops Lavender essential oil.
- 5 drops of Rose essential oil.

This recipe is for a medium to large sized dog and is to be used straight. Combine the oils listed and rub the oil into the affected area. Prevent your dog from licking off the blend for 15 to 20 minutes, either by holding the animal or by wrapping the area.

24. Aging Care

All dogs get older and need extra support. This recipe is helpful for the aging process.

Start with 3 table spoons of coconut oil or other carrier oil (for a medium sized dog. If your needs are different, use the Dilution guide in this book).

Ingredients:

- 3 drops of Lavender
- 3 drops of Peppermint
- 2 drops of Copaiba
- 2 drops of balsam fir

This can be made into an ointment to rub directly on the area of concern or applied to the pad of the foot for faster absorption into the blood stream.

25. Sinus Infections

Dogs with sinus infection or other respiratory problems have nasal congestion and perhaps difficulty breathing. This blend can relieve nasal congestion and can be used in several ways.

Ingredients:

- 2 oz. (60 ml) base oil (e.g. fractionated coconut oil)
- 4 drops of Eucalyptus
- 2 drops of Myrhh
- 1 drop of Niaouli

The carrier oil guideline is for a medium to large sized dog. To edit this recipe for your dog's size and age, use the Dilution guide in this book. Store in a dark glass bottle.

Several drops can be massaged into the fur of the dog's neck and chest, or placed on a cloth bandanna, or several drops can be added to the dog's bedding. Another good way to decongest the sinuses is to bring the dog into the bathroom when you are showering. Let the dog lay on the floor. Drop 6 to 10 drops of the blend onto the floor of the shower. The combination of the steam and vaporized oils can greatly clear sinus congestion. Finally, you can add the essential oils (without the base oil) to a diffuser and diffuse the oils for 5 minutes at a time up to several times a day.

26. Pet Salve

This brilliant recipe is great for burns, skin irritation and dry cracked paws. It can be applied directly to the affected area as needed.

Ingredients:

- 1 Cup Organic Virgin Coconut Oil
- 1 Cup Organic Extra Virgin Olive Oil
- 4 Tablespoon Beeswax Pastilles
- *Per 4 ounce jar (4 to 5 four ounce glass jars):*
- 12 drops Lavender
- 12 drops Frankincense
- 1/2 teaspoon vitamin E oil (*optional*)

Instructions:

- Add the coconut and olive oil along with beeswax to a wide mouth mason jar or a 4 cup glass pyrex measuring bowl. Set glass container in a pan of simmering water. Stir occasionally, more stirring towards the end as the beeswax will float to the top.
- Set out jars to fill, add essential oils listed to EACH jar. Next, pour melted oils into the jars over the essential oils, you can stir the oils in but they should mix nicely without stirring. Fill to 1/4 inch from the top. Cover with a paper towel and cool on counter for at least 8 hours before sealing with lid. Shelf life without the vitamin e oils is approximately 4 to 5 months.

This recipe can be used for any age dog, but check with a health professional if your pet is very young, very old or suffers from sensitive skin.

27. Dry Skin

This essential oil recipe is great for helping your dog with its dry skin.

Ingredients:

- 1 tablespoon organic Argan oil.
- 10 drops German Chamomile essential oil.

Directions:

Combine oils and rub into the affected area. Prevent animal from licking off the blend for 15 to 20 minutes, either by holding the animal or by wrapping the area. This recipe can be used for any age dog, but check with a health professional if your pet is very young, very old or suffers from sensitive skin.

28. Flea Repellent

You can either add the following recipe to 8 oz. (240 ml) of an all-natural shampoo to make a flea-repellent shampoo or to 2 oz. of a base oil to make an oil blend.

Ingredients:

- 2 drops Citronella
- 1-2 drops Lemon
- 1-2 drops Clary Sage
- 2-3 drops of Peppermint

Apply a few drops of the oil blend to the neck, back, chest, legs, and tail of your dog. You can also add a few drops to your dog's cotton collar or bandanna to make an aromatic flea collar. This recipe can be used for any age dog, but check with a health professional if your pet is very young, very old or suffers from sensitive skin.

Single Neem oil is also effective flea and mosquito repellent.

29. Neck Collar Protection

This essential oil blend is great for protecting your dog.

Ingredients:

- 5 drops Vetiver essential oil
- 5 drops Lemon eucalyptus essential oil
- 10 drops Sandalwood essential oil

Mix together all ingredients, and rub into the top side of your pet's collar. Make sure the collar is tight enough so that the pet cannot lick it. This recipe can be used for any age dog, but check with a health professional if your pet is very young, very old or suffers from sensitive skin. Note that this blend may stain the pet collar!

30. Mosquito Repellent

This is an effective mosquito (or fleas) repellent. If you live in a place where mosquitoes are common, you need to protect your dog from mosquitoes since they transmit the heartworm disease.

Ingredients:

- 7 drops of Citronella
- 5 drops of Lemongrass
- 5 drops of Rose Geranium
- 10 drops of Myrrh
- 8 ounces of Aloe Vera juice

Spritz this blend on your dog's coat every day (avoid eye areas). You can also spray this around doorways and on bedding to repel pests. This recipe can be used for any age dog, but check with a health professional if your pet is very young, very old or suffers from sensitive skin.

31. Dog Burns

Cool the burn with a cold water compress and then apply Lavender essential oil as soon as possible. Silver Shield Rescue gel can also be used.

This recipe can be used for any age dog, but check with a health professional if your pet is very young, very old or suffers from sensitive skin.

32. Bad Breath Biscuits

A successful way to help with your dogs' bad breath in a way that they will enjoy.

Makes about 1 dozen biscuits for large dogs or 2-3 dozen for small dogs. Start by preheating the oven to 350 F

- 2 cups Coconut Flour (or gluten free mix flour works too)
- 1/2 cup Oats (gluten free)
- 1/4 tsp Salt (option– will help to preserve the biscuits)
- 1/4 tsp Cinnamon (do not use pumpkin pie spice because dogs do not tolerate nutmeg)
- 2 Bananas
- 2 TBSP Peanut/Almond/Sunflower Seed butter
- 2 TBSP Coconut Oil
- 3 Eggs
- Peppermint Essential Oil
    - Toy breeds: 3 drops
    - Small dogs: 4 drops
    - Medium dogs: 6 drops
    - Large dogs: 8+ drops

Mix the dry ingredients (flour, oats and cinnamon spice) in a mixing bowl. Set aside. In another bowl mix the bananas, nut butter, coconut oil and eggs until thoroughly incorporated. Add the essential oil and stir to combine.

Mix the dry ingredients slowly into the wet ingredients until combined. The dough is a bit crumbly – this is fine and to be expected. You can add a bit more banana if you need to get it to hold together better.

Place the dough over floured wax paper and roll out until you get the height you want your dog biscuits to be – roughly 1/4 inch. Use a knife or a cookie cutter to cut the shapes you would like and place them on a cookie sheet.

Put the dog biscuits into the oven for 20-30 minutes (depending on the size of the cut outs). Place them on a cookie rack to cool and they will become even crispier.

33. Hyperactivity

This aromatherapy recipe is effective for calming hyperactive dogs.

Ingredients:

- 2 oz. (60 ml) base oil (e.g. olive oil, fractionated coconut oil, jojoba oil)
- 3 drops Valerian
- 3 drops Lavender
- 2 drops Roman Chamomile
- 2 drops Sweet Marjoram
- 1 drops Bergamot

This recipe is for medium sized dogs. If your needs very, use the Dilution guide in this book to determine how much carrier oil you'll need.

Use this blend topically on your dog. Rub 2 to 3 drops of the essential oil blend between your hands and apply it on the edge of your dog's ears, between the toes, on his inner thighs, or under his "armpits".

34. Tear staining

Lavender essential oil is a natural solution for tear staining.

Once a day, put a drop or less in the palm of your hand then use the index finger to apply the drop by rubbing your finger across the upper bridge of your dog's nose right below its eyes, where the tear stains are. Lavender unblocks the eye ducts and kills the bacteria caused by the tearing.

Lavender is also great for any eye issues, e.g. injuries. 8 drops of Lavender should be mixed to 8 ounce of steamed distilled water and a packet of sodium chloride/sodium bicarbonate ups grade (1/2 of a teaspoon). The blend must be shaken each time before use if you do not use an emulsifier. The mix is similar to eyewash solutions used for humans. Put the mixture in a glass spray bottle and spray it 2-3 times in the affected eye once per day and watch the healing begin.

35. Keep Off the Furniture

The scent of this breezy fabric spray doesn't just freshen furniture, carpet and drapes, it may give dogs pause before going where they shouldn't.

Ingredients:

- 5 teaspoons Lavender essential oil
- 5 teaspoons Peppermint essential oil
- 5 teaspoons Lemon essential oil
- 32 ounces of water

Directions:

1. Place essential oils in a clean, empty 32 ounce spray bottle.
2. Fill bottle with water and cap tightly with the sprayer.
3. Shake contents vigorously and apply 2 to 3 sprays to target area.
4. Repeat as necessary.

This recipe can be used for any age dog, but check with a health professional if your pet is very young, very old or suffers from sensitive skin.

36. Asthma

There is a recipe that is great for dogs with asthma or breathing difficulties. The *ingredients* in this blend are:

- Eucalyptus globules
- Eucalyptus citriodora
- Myrtle
- Eucalyptus radiate
- Peppermint (India)
- Spruce
- Ravintsara
- Pine
- Sweet Marjoram

This recipe can be used for small to extra large sized dogs and is to be used aromatically. Use the <u>Dilution</u> chapter of this book to edit the blend to suit your needs.

37. Insomnia

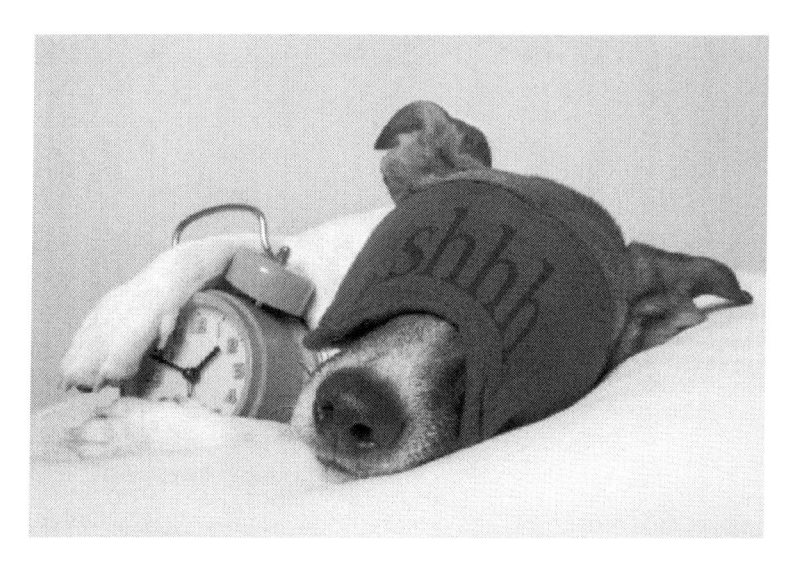

Lack of sleep can be very troubling for dogs. To help with this, you should diffuse a few drops of any of these oils (or a combination of 2 or 3) to use aromatically where your dog sleeps:

- Lavender
- Roman Chamomile
- Clary Sage
- Sweet Marjoram
- Valerian

This is suitable for dogs of any age and size, but check with a health professional if your dog is very young, very old or suffers from sensitive skin.

38. Immune Support for Environmental and Seasonal Threats

- Place one drop of Lavender, Lemon and Peppermint in an empty capsule and give it to dog, or put in food.
- Because dogs are carnivores, their diet needs to be grain free. 95% of allergies are caused by diet. Homemade or raw food diet is recommended.

This is suitable for dogs of any age and size, but check with a health professional if your dog is very young or very old.

39. Tooth Decay

There is a blend called **Thieves** from Young Living, which is excellent for helping to prevent tooth decay.

In a 4-ounce glass spray bottle, mix 2 drops of thieves to 1 ounce of steamed distilled water. It's best to use the blend at night to spray on your dog's upper gums and teeth. Lift the upper lip on each side of your dog's mouth and spray the mix on the teeth. Thieves kills the bacteria that cause the tooth decay. It also makes your dog's immune system stronger, it is a natural antibiotic. Antibiotics made from drugs kill both - the bad and the good bacteria. Thieves solution is a cheaper, easier and healthier method of daily brushing their teeth or bringing your dog in to the vet for the recommended 6-month teeth cleaning.

40. First Aid Kit

Finally, the following oils are recommended as a first aid kit for your dog, as they are useful for emergencies:

- Lavender Essential Oil
- Melrose Essential Oil
- Peppermint Essential Oils
- Helichrysum Essential Oil

ESSENTIAL OILS FOR COMMON DOG AILMENTS

Ailment	Essential Oils to Use
Allergies	Lemon, Peppermint, Lavender
Arthritis	Peppermint and Frankincense, Helichrysum, Ginger
Asthma	Eucalyptus globules, Myrtle, Eucalyptus Radiate, Pine, Marjoram, Peppermint
Bleeding	Helichrysum or Lemon
Bleeding Toe Nail	Lemon or Helichrysum
Bladder Infection	Frankincense
Breathing Issues	Balsam fir (Idaho), Eucalyptus Radiate
Burns	Lavender
Calming	Lavender, Roman Chamomile, Marjoram, Bergamot
Cancer (Tumours)	Frankincense

Diabetes	Basil and/or Coriander, Lavender
Diarrhea	Peppermint, Roman Chamomile
Dry Skin	Clary Sage, German Chamomile
Ear Infection	Geranium and/or Frankincense and/or Basil, Bergamot, Lavender, Roman Chamomile, Niaouli
Fear/Anxiety/Nervousness	Lavender
Fleas	Lemon, Clary Sage, Peppermint
Fever	Peppermint
Fungal Infection	Lavender, Geranium, Lemongrass and/or Clary sage
Gallstones/Infection	Frankincense and Lemon
Heart Problems	Peppermint
Hot Spots	Lavender
Infection (Systemic)	Helichrysum, Lavender, Geranium and/or Marjoram
Infections (Wound)	Frankincense, Helichrysum
Insect Bite/Sting	Basic and Lavender, German Chamomile, Eucalyptus
Insect Repellent	Peppermint
Insomnia	Lavender, Roman Chamomile, Clary Sage, Marjoram
Internal Parasites	Peppermint, Lemongrass
Interstitial Cysts	Lavender
Itchiness	Lavender, Roman Chamomile, Frankincense

Joint Pain	Idaho Balsam fir, Helichrysum, Peppermint
Liver/Gallbladder disorders	Geranium and/or Helichrysum
Mosquitoes	Peppermint, Geranium, Myrrh, Lemongrass
Motion Sickness	Peppermint, Ginger
Mouth Abscess/ Gum Disease/ Oral Surgery/ Dental	Lavender, Clove
Nausea/Vomiting	Peppermint, Lavender, Ginger
Pain	Peppermint and Frankincense, Lavender, Balsam Fir (Idaho)
Parvo	Oregano
Respiratory Infections	Eucalyptus Radiate, Pine
Scar	Frankincense, Helichrysum
Seizures	Frankincense
Separations Anxiety	Lavender
Shock	Peppermint
Sinus Infections	Eucalyptus, Myrrh, Niaouli, Geranium, Lavender
Skin Allergies/ Rash/ Dermatitis/ Irritations	Lavender, Helichrysum, Roman Chamomile
Stress/Anxiety/Fears	Lavender
Stroke	Frankincense, Lavender
Ticks	Lavender, Geranium, Eucalyptus
Toxins	Roman Chamomile, Lavender

Tumours	Frankincense
Urinary Tract Stones/Crystals	Lemon, Frankincense
Vomiting	Peppermint
Worms	Peppermint
Wounds	Frankincense, Helichrysum, Marjoram, Lavender

RECAP - TOP 20 TIPS FOR ESSENTIAL OILS USE WITH DOGS

Now that we've covered all of the basics for essential oil usage with your pets, it's time to recap with a list of the Top 20 most important pieces of information you'll need:

1. Essential oils are non toxic, easy to use and easy to make, making them the perfect home remedy for your dog. Having some on hand at all times, means your dog won't have to suffer any common ailment for very long!

2. Essential oils can be applied in one of 3 ways: topically, internally or aromatically. The recommended way will ensure the oil works in the quickest, safest and most effective way.
3. Always use therapeutic grade essential oils for use with your dog. It's important to remember that these oils are the safest ones for your pet.
4. Always research essential oils before you use them. The more knowledge you have on the oil you're using, the less chance you will make any mistakes.
5. 'Pure' oils are undiluted, whereas 'quality' oils are made by a decent manufacturer – don't mix up the two.
6. The way you dilute your essential oils is very dependent on your dog's age and size. There is a guide to this included in this book, but if you're ever unsure, speak to a medical professional.
7. Store your essential oils in a cool, dark place out of the reach of children or animals to prevent poisoning or overdose. Sometimes the color of the bottle your oil is kept in will affect the oils quality, so always take the time to put some research into this.
8. It is best to prevent prolonged use of the same essential oil as a tolerance can build up, rendering it ineffective.
9. There is a *Pet Poison Helpline* (800-213-6680), if you are ever worried about your dog.
10. Dogs will decide if they like essential oils by their sense of smell. Some people believe that they can even pick out exactly what they need in this way. Don't ever force inhalation by use of a muzzle.
11. Tea tree is considered dangerous for dogs, so to be on the safe side, it is best to avoid use.
12. Don't immediately think that if something is going well, it's best to increase the dose. The recommended guidelines suggest that you should use the least amount of oil possible, as long as it is having a positive effect. Less is more.
13. Some essential oil users recommend petting as the most effective way of applying topically.
14. When blending oils, for a nice scent, it is best to use the 30 – 50 – 20 method. 30% top note (strong smelling), 50% middle not and 20% base note. Smell is important to dogs, so these guidelines are very useful.
15. When showing a new essential oil to your dog, assess its reaction before use. If it smells and licks the oil, that's a positive reaction.
16. If you see any of the signs of poisoning – vomiting, walking funny, struggling to breathe, etc – contact a professional immediately. The quicker you act, the quicker you dog will recover.
17. Never apply essential oils directly to an animal's muzzle area, inside nostrils, ears or mouth, and genital areas.

18. Use the online resources available to contact other pet owners who use essential oils. The tips, advice and recipes they can give you will be invaluable.
19. The National Association for Holistic Aromatherapy (naha.org) has conducted studies on this very topic, so you'll be able to find out all kinds of useful information from their website.
20. Essential oils have been used for centuries – on humans and animals. It can't hurt your dog to try them. Who knows, you might find yourself reverting completely and never looking back!

FAQ

1. Are essential oils safe for dogs?

Some sources, e.g. www.experience-essential-oils.com suggest that *all* home remedies for dogs should include essential oils. Dogs respond really well to the treatments essential oils offer and they can be used safely for everything, from fleas to bumps and bruises.

2. What is the difference between essential oils and aromatherapy?

Aromatherapy is defined as:

"Aromatherapy is the therapeutic use of plant-derived, aromatic essential oils to promote physical and psychological well-being. It is sometimes used in combination with massage and other therapeutic techniques as part of a holistic treatment approach."

So it's the practice of using essential oils in massage. **The Blissful Dog** (theblissfuldog.com/aromatherapy-for-dogs) gives a great guide to aromatherapy and dogs.

3. Can I use essential oils for my dog paws?

Paws are a great place to apply topical essential oils because they are an easy and absorbent surface. Below is a useful set of instructions for doing this.

Canine Reflexology Chart

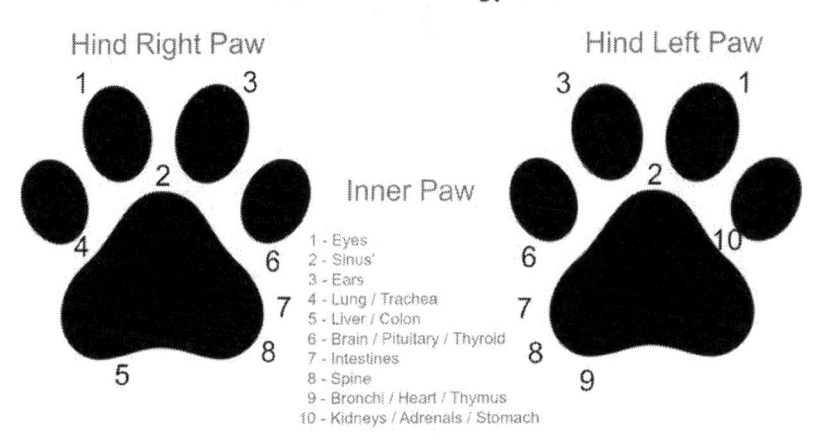

Hind Right Paw   **Hind Left Paw**

Inner Paw

1 - Eyes
2 - Sinus'
3 - Ears
4 - Lung / Trachea
5 - Liver / Colon
6 - Brain / Pituitary / Thyroid
7 - Intestines
8 - Spine
9 - Bronchi / Heart / Thymus
10 - Kidneys / Adrenals / Stomach

4. Does the ratios of essential oils matter based on dog size and age?

Yes the ratio of oils does depend on a number of factors including the dog's size and age. Recipes will often give you a guide in reference to this, and you can also check the <u>Dilution</u> chapter for more information.

5. Where are the most common places for buying essential oil blends?

There are many online resources for buying essential oil blends. These include Young Living.com, doTerra.com, EdensGarden.com, Amazon.com and iHerb.com to name a few. You will also be able to gain assistance from your local pet care store.

6. Are there any clinical studies to prove the healing properties of essential oils for dogs?

There have been some clinical studies conducted which clearly demonstrate the healing properties of essential oils for dogs, such as the NCBI (http://www.ncbi.nlm.nih.gov/pubmed/24355814), and there are many more in progress. As it becomes a more popular concept, more scientists want to look into it.

7. How do you clean your pet's ears using essential oils?

Therapeutic Grade Essential Oils are great for cleaning your dog's ears as they don't contain any synthetic materials or compounds. Lavender is the most commonly used oil for ear cleaning, so that has been used in the guide below:

Use about 3-5 drops of lavender with about a teaspoon of V-6 oil. This is usually good for about two or three cleanings depending on how big and dirty your dog's ears are. It's best to make it up and keep it in a dark oil bottle that way the oil doesn't degrade and go bad.

Then place several drops on the cotton swab and remove the surface dirt and wax. Make sure that you don't stick the swab down into the ear canal. This easy technique will have your dog's ears cleaned in no time!

8. How do you treat ear mites using essential oils?

Below is an extensive list of possible symptoms for ear mites in dogs:

- Head shaking
- Scratching and rubbing of ears
- Inflammation of the ear
- Dark colored waxy secretion
- Strong odor
- Hair loss or dermatitis

To treat this, it is recommended using Diluted Oregon Oil or Mullein Oil which can be used to saturate a cotton wool ball and used to clean out the dog's ears, removing any excess debris as you go.

9. What is the best way to dilute essential oils to use for your dogs?

It is suggested that the dilution is all about the size of the dog and the following guidelines are recommended:

- Dogs 10 pounds and under, dilute essential oil with 75% + carrier oil.
- Dogs 11-25 pounds, dilute essential oil with 75% carrier oil.
- Dogs 26-46 pounds, dilute essential oil with 50-75% carrier oil.
- Dogs 46-75 pounds, dilute essential oil with 50% carrier oil.
- Dogs 76-90 pounds, dilute essential oil with 25-50% carrier oil.
- Dogs 91-150 pounds, dilute essential oil with 25% carrier oil.
- Dogs > 150 pounds, dilute essential oil with 0-25% carrier oil.

You also need to consider the dog's age in your dilution techniques, as explained in the Dilution chapter of this book.

Of course, you should always consult your vet before using any ratio of essential oils.

10. How do you effectively avoid the wrong essential oils that may put your dog in danger?

You have seen in this book the signs of poisoning and a list of potentially bad oils, so it is best to always keep this in mind when treating your dog. If you have any questions at all, speak to your health professional – they can give you unique, specific advice based on your pets circumstances.

11. How can I make a herbal flea collar for dogs using essential oils?

Below is a brilliant recipe for creating your very own flea collar for your dog using essential oils:

Ingredients:

- 1/2 teaspoon Rubbing Alcohol
- 1 drop Cedarwood Essential Oil
- 1 drop Lavender Essential Oil
- 1 drop Citronella Essential Oil
- 1 drop Thyme Essential Oil
- 4 garlic oil capsules

Directions:

- Get any collar that's made of material (i.e. no chains) and soak it in the above mixture.
- Lay it out to dry.
- Once it's dry, place it on your animal's neck.
- Repeat process at least once per month.

12. Is it safe for dogs to lick aromatherapy oils?

The **Animal Aromatherapy and Essential Oil Safety** (http://www.ncbi.nlm.nih.gov/pubmed/24355814) report gives the following statement:

"Do not give essential oils internally to your pets/animal clients. Animals will often lick the area where essential oil blends/botanicals have been applied. This normally does not cause a problem – but watch to make sure that the animal does not have an allergic reaction, or negative response. If they do, wipe the area with a cool wet cloth and diluted mild soap, rinse and repeat. If necessary seek immediate veterinarian assistance.

Other and more serious clinical signs to watch for with your pet that can result from ingestion of essential oils are: vomiting, diarrhea, depression, lethargy, weakness, excessive drooling/salivation, mouth sores, seizures, tremors, increase in liver enzymes and temporary paralysis."

13. Is it safe to put a couple of drops of essential peppermint oil in your dog's water bowl?

Many sources recommend adding the drops of essential peppermint oils in your dog's water bowl to ensure that they take it correctly.

14. Is tea tree oil toxic to dogs?

There is a lot of research to suggest that tea tree oil is toxic to dogs and must be avoided. The Pet Poison Helpline (www.petpoisonhelpline.com) has issued this statement on the matter:

"Tea tree oil, also known as melaleuca oil, is an essential oil produced from the Australian tea tree plant (Melaleuca alternifolia). Tea tree oil is known for its antifungal and antibacterial properties, and possibly for its antipruritic, anti-inflammatory, and antiparasitic effects. Tea tree oil is often found in varying concentrations and high concentrations should never be used on pets. As little as 7 drops of 100% oil has resulted in severe poisoning, and applications of 10-20 mls of 100% oil have resulted in poisoning and death in both dogs and cats. Products containing tea tree oil concentrations less than 1-2% are generally considered non-toxic if used according to labeled directions. Clinical signs include a low body temperature, weakness, walking drunk, inability to walk, tremors, coma, increased liver enzymes, and even death."

It warns pet owners to look out for the symptoms/reactions described, and suggests that for the safety of your pet, avoid use of tea tree oil at all costs.

15. How can you avoid the common mistakes in essential oil usage?

Below is a list of suggestions that will help you avoid any mistakes when it comes to using essential oils with your pet:

- *Knowledge is key* – the more you know about the essential oil you're using, the less chance you'll have of making any errors.
- *Awareness* – knowing that essential oils shouldn't leave a greasy residue or that price = quality, will ensure you pick a better product.
- *Care* – using essential oils around the home *can* cause an overdose if you're also using them topically with your pet.

RESOURCES

YOUNG LIVING
ESSENTIAL OILS

www.youngliving.com

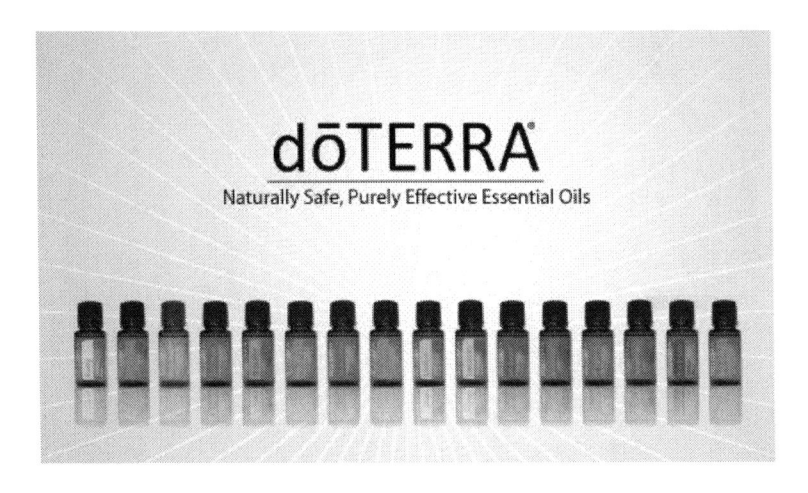

dōTERRA
Naturally Safe, Purely Effective Essential Oils

www.doterra.com

www.weedemandreap.com

www.iherb.com

thebark.com

www.wag.com

ESSENTIAL OILS FOR DOGS

DogsNaturally
the magazine for dogs without boundaries

www.dogsnaturallymagazine.com

HOPEWELL ESSENTIAL OILS

hopewelloils.com

PLANT THERAPY®
100% PURE ESSENTIAL OILS

www.planttherapy.com

Healthy pets
With Dr. Karen Becker
Presented by Mercola.com

healthypets.mercola.com

www.rockymountainoils.com

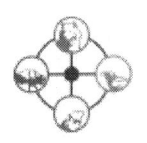

www.nativeamericannutritionals.com

www.viovet.co.uk

www.mountainroseherbs.com

Aura Cacia

pure aromatherapy

www.auracacia.com

STARWEST BOTANICALS

www.starwest-botanicals.com

Edens Garden

100% PURE AROMATHERAPY

www.edensgarden.com

CONCLUSION

So as this guide has clearly demonstrated, **using essential oils in your dog's healthcare is a non-toxic, easy way to ensure that they stay healthy.** There are so many benefits it's easy to see why more and more people are turning to these alternative treatments.

Not only are these remedies an all-natural, more affordable alternative to traditional medication, they are also easy to make yourself at home – as demonstrated by the remedies available in this guide, so why not give it a go yourself?

It isn't just your pet that has to benefit from your new found love of essential oils – you can too, and not just your health. Check out *101 Uses For Essential Oils* at http://draxe.com/essential-oil-uses-benefits for plenty of tips and advice. Once you've seen how dramatic the benefits to you can be, you won't' look back.

This book has given you the basics, but if you'd like to speak to other dog owners who use essential oils, to discuss stories, swap recipes, etc then here are a few online forums to get you started:

Dog Forum at www.dogforum.com

Dogster at www.dogster.com

Spoiled Maltese at spoiledmaltese.com/forum/52-maltese-health-behavior/223722-essential-oils-pets.html

Good luck with your essential oils usage for yourself and your pet!

ABOUT THE AUTHOR

Mary Jones became interested in herbal remedies early on in her life. She came to essential oils after years of looking for solutions to her problems in the medical world. Issues like allergies, weight loss, and lack of energy didn't really seem to have good solutions in the traditional medicine. There were expensive treatments to be had, but often they did not work in the long term and were not as holistic as Mary wanted the treatments to be.

In her search for a solution, she came upon essential oils and aromatherapy. As she had learned about the stress relieving power of aromatherapy, she began intensely studying essential oils–how they work, how they are used, how they are made, which are safe to use, and beyond. She traveled to study with those who had long used essential oils and taught others about the many uses. For decades, she has developed her knowledge about this subject.

One of Mary's life goals is to make the world a better, happier place, and her writings are definitely a testament to that. She has not just kept all of her research and discoveries to herself. She has elected to share them, in a format that makes them available to just about everyone.

Now, after years of compiling information about the most beneficial and useful essential oils, Mary has written several books to introduce others to the knowledge she has gathered.

Printed in Great Britain
by Amazon